Beating Them All!
Thirty Days to a Magic Score on
Any Elementary Literacy Instruction
Exam for Teacher Certification

BEATING THEM ALL!
Thirty Days to a Magic Score on Any Elementary Literacy Instruction Exam for Teacher Certification

RICA CSET AEPA MTTC
ICTS TExES/ExCET NYSTC
OPTE/OSAT MTEL MRTT PLACE

CHRIS NICHOLAS BOOSALIS

Boston ■ New York ■ San Francisco
Mexico City ■ Montreal ■ Toronto ■ London ■ Madrid ■ Munich ■ Paris
Hong Kong ■ Singapore ■ Tokyo ■ Cape Town ■ Sydney

Series Editor: *Aurora Martínez Ramos*
Editorial Assistant: *Erin Beatty*
Senior Marketing Manager: *Elizabeth Fogarty*
Production Editor: *Michelle Limoges*
Compositor: *Omegatype Typography, Inc.*
Composition and Prepress Buyer: *Linda Cox*
Manufacturing Buyer: *Andrew Turso*
Cover Designer: *Kristina Mose-Libon*

For related titles and support materials, visit our online catalog at www.ablongman.com.

This book offers expert and reliable information regarding the reading exams and reading instruction content covered. It is sold with the understanding that the purchaser/user will verify all of the information about these exams and will also recognize that no promise of success could ever reasonably accompany the purchase/use of this book. The author and publisher specifically disclaim any liability that is incurred from any and all types of use/misuse and/or application/misapplication of the contents of this book.

The terms RICA, CSET, AEPA, MTTC, ICTS, TExES/ExCET, NYSTC, OPTE/OSAT, MTEL, MRTT, and PLACE are all registered trademarks of National Evaluation Systems, Inc.

Library of Congress Cataloging-in-Publication Data

CIP data not available at the time of publication.

0-205-39472-8

Printed in the United States of America

10 9 8 7 6 5 4 3 2 1   07 06 05 04 03

This book is dedicated to the courageous and dedicated women and men who want to teach children and to everyone who is involved with their preparation.

CONTENTS

CHAPTER SIX
The Magic Plan   144

Official Site: http://www.ablongman.com/boosalis

PREFACE

This book offers serious preparation for serious candidates. It is designed to provide comprehensive and in-depth support to test takers, college instructors, and preparation leaders alike. This text addresses everything that you must know prior to the exam, including the secrets of a passing score (Chapter 1), the reading-instruction content that you must know cold (Chapter 2), the strategies for data analysis and the written portions (Chapter 3), the strategies for data analysis and the multiple-choice portions (Chapter 4), essential time management models (Chapter 5), and a thirty-day study plan to ensure that you are as prepared as you can be before test day (Chapter 6).

Here is how this book helps all people who are involved with these exams.

- *Test Takers.* Preparing for these exams is often challenging and worrisome. There is a lot of information to learn in a very short amount of time, not to mention the daunting format of the test faced under strict time restrictions. The singular goal of this text is to ensure that you learn *what to know* before the test and practice *what to do* on the day of the test. Understanding what to know and do for your exam definitely increases your chances of passing on the first attempt.

  The book helps you because it teaches you everything that you need to know to be successful, from the underlying score that is really required to pass, to the strategies that you need to understand to complete all of the formats under timed conditions, to content that is aligned with the exam and that can be learned in thirty days. The book's method of study is outlined in chapter 6. Following this method ensures that you know everything that a candidate possibly could know prior to testing and that a passing score is well within reach after this essential preparation.

- *College Instructors.* The book offers you a way to ensure that your students have "covered the material" that is most often tested on the exam. As you know, your class time and autonomy are being consumed by these high-stakes exams because of their impact on your students' lives and futures. The book provides you and your students with the opportunity to learn the core content of this reading instruction model while you carry out activities and use materials that you know are important for a future teacher to know—but that may not be tested on the exam. The book also handles material that may not be to your philosophical liking, but that must be covered anyway because "it's on the test." This text reduces the burden that these exams place on your shoulders so that you can return to the real profession of preparing future teachers to teach real children to read, not just to pass a state exam of reading instruction.

- *Preparation Leaders.* Test preparation leaders provide an essential link between candidates and these high-stakes tests. The book is written to be immediately practical to candidates and to those charged with preparing them. The examples and explanations are clear, and the content is easily incorporated into any existing framework of preparation. The goal is to help you to help others through time management models, essential strategies, aligned content, and activities that incorporate state standards for reading (K–8), all of which make preparation both comprehensive and easy. Three years of research went into producing *Beating Them All!* to ensure that its preparation format is truly the best available.

WHAT TESTS DOES THIS BOOK COVER?

The book addresses the reading-instruction content for the following exams:

- Arizona Educator Proficiency Assessments (AEPA–Elementary, Reading portion of Elementary Education)
- California Reading Instruction Competence Assessment (RICA)
- California Subject Examinations for Teachers (CSETMSCP—Subtest 1: Reading)
- Texas Master Reading Teacher Test (MRTT)*
- Certification Examinations for Oklahoma Educators (OPTE–Early Childhood, Elementary, Middle, and OSAT–Reading Specialist)
- Massachusetts Tests for Educator Licensure (MTEL–Reading)
- Program for Licensing Assessments for Colorado Educators (PLACE–Elementary Education, Early Childhood Education, Reading Teacher)
- New York State Teacher Certification Exam (NYSTCE/ATS–Written)
- Texas Examinations of Educator Standards (TExES)/Texas Examination for the Certification of Educators in Texas (ExCET) (Reading and reading instruction portions of Reading/Reading Specialist)
- Michigan MTTC (Reading and reading instruction portions of Elementary)
- Illinois Certification Testing System (ICTS–Reading, Early Childhood, Elementary)

WHAT CONTENT DOES THIS BOOK COVER?

This is the core body of reading-instruction content that is tested on all of these exams. Following are the areas that are covered exhaustively in Chapter 2.

Assessment principles
- Individual and group assessments in reading

Decoding instruction
- Concepts about print
- Phonemic awareness
- Phonics instruction
- Spelling instruction

*This book is useful for the content of this exam, although additional reading is required for the mentoring content that is assessed.

Fluency instruction
- Teacher-directed instruction
- Independent reading

Reading comprehension instruction
- Vocabulary development
- Reading comprehension strategies
- Narrative text comprehension
- Content-area literacy

Oral and written language development
- Oral and written language development
- Organization, style, and grammar

Classroom planning
- Selecting texts
- Writing units
- Managing groups

This list captures the core content that all candidates must know prior to the exam. The text covers it in a way that makes pure test preparation both comprehensive and effective for the purpose of passing the test. Furthermore, this core content is easily adapted to incorporate any literacy model, whether it occurs within this framework or directly opposes it. This way, no one needs to worry about whether he or she has covered the test material at the expense of real-world instruction.

WHY DO I NEED THIS BOOK FOR MY PREPARATION?

Experience shows that candidates fail these exams for three reasons:

1. No goal for obtaining a passing score
2. No knowledge of the content that is appropriate for the exam
3. No strategies to handle the written or multiple-choice questions, and no methods to manage time on the test overall

These exams require truly require comprehensive preparation. The more that candidates know about the test and what to do on the day of it, the better their chances of passing on the first attempt. Here is how it works. First, the book covers the underlying score that candidates need to know while doing the test. That score is *the magic score*. Next, the text covers the content that aligns well with the test in a way that makes preparation easy. Finally, candidates are taught strategies to beat the written and multiple-choice questions that test a person's knowledge of the content of Chapter 2, along with teaching candidates concrete methods for making their test work for them under time conditions. This way, the major reasons for failure are not issues for candidates who use this text as their primary source of test preparation.

HOW IS THIS BOOK STRUCTURED?

The structure of the text offers comprehensive preparation to candidates. Here is a chapter-by-chapter account of this text.

- Chapter 1: This chapter details the exams that candidates face and how these exams are scored. Then, it presents the underlying *magic score* required to pass. Finally, the chapter gives an overview of the core reading-instruction model that is taught in Chapter 2.
- Chapter 2: This chapter covers the core model of reading instruction in depth. Candidates learn all about assessments and activities in literacy instruction that align well with the content tested most often on these exams. The format of this chapter makes transferring the content of this chapter to both the written and multiple-choice portions of these exams easy and successful.
- Chapter 3: This chapter presents the major essay formats that many candidates experience on test day. It also covers essential data analysis methods and question formats that all candidates must learn, regardless of whether their test has essays on it. Because the formats of many of the questions mirror the essays described in this chapter, the text shows a way to help all candidates *write their way to a passing score*—regardless of what their exam looks like.
- Chapter 4: This chapter offers effective methods to handle the multiple-choice questions through strategies. It also teaches candidates how to use simple data analysis models to analyze the multiple-choice questions quickly and effectively. No other preparation manuals show candidates how to be truly effective on these types of questions in the way *Beating Them All* does. Its methods are truly unique and revolutionary.
- Chapter 5: This chapter addresses the major time management models developed for the exams described in Chapter 1. Special methods exist for completing the exams under timed conditions. Furthermore, there are ways to make the exams work to the candidate's advantage instead of to his or her disadvantage. This chapter is a very valuable and eye-opening read for anyone involved with these exams. In short, it shows the candidate how to beat the test by using the test against itself.
- Chapter 6: This chapter outlines a four-week study plan that carries candidates from their first day of study to the day of the test. The plan is flexible and can be modified to suit different schedules. It ensures that readers learn the content of Chapter 2 (see Appendix A), the essential standards from the state (see Appendix B), and the most important data analysis procedures that are necessary for the exam (see Appendix C). It should now be obvious that the book offers comprehensive study that is manageable, effective, and powerful.

IS OUTSIDE READING REQUIRED?

As with other preparation manuals, outside reading is encouraged. That reading can come from methods courses, the journals listed in the bibliography of this book, or from other selected sources. Journals were purposely selected. They are easy to locate at university libraries. Instructors can also place them on reserve for students to use in their preparation. The state standards for literacy instruction are also an important part of the preparation since many of the exams are sensitive to them. Please also visit http://www.ablongman.com/ boosalis for the most up-to-date information on your test, additional readings, and other items of interest that are related to your preparation.

WHERE IS THE SAMPLE EXAM?

Unlike other preparation manuals, this one does not offer anyone a sample exam. It differs from other preparation sources in a very important and fundamental way: *It is honest.*

Research demonstrates that practicing on contrived sample exams, especially the multiple-choice portions, is not only ineffective but harmful. The items that other manuals include really are nothing more than someone's "best guess" about what the items will be like. Practicing on those items only gives you a false sense of security. Worse, candidates may develop bad habits and grow accustomed to reading item formats that won't appear on the actual exam at all. If you do a little online reading about other preparation manuals and what candidates say about them, you will see this in a very short time.

Therefore, the only practice exams that this text endorses and demands that you locate and purchase are the ones that come from the company that developed your test itself. The study guide for your exam may be available online. Visit http://www.ablongman.com/ boosalis for links to your state's department of education or go directly to the test's official site for information on how to download it. Also, many of the guides can be ordered through the mail (usually under $10 apiece and with quick delivery). These forms are available in most registration bulletins. Restrictions may apply regarding who can download or mail order these materials, so check the sites and read the bulletins carefully.

Please get started on obtaining these guides sooner rather than later. If you do nothing else, these guides will be the second essential ingredient in your success—the first will be reaching your magic score!

ACKNOWLEDGMENTS

I am very grateful to my friends at Allyn & Bacon who made this project possible. Their efforts to provide assistance to teacher credential candidates through quality literature must be acknowledged. I am especially thankful to my editor, Aurora Martinez, for her support of, and commitment to, this project, and to her assistant, Katie Freddoso, whose efforts made the writing of this book smooth and enjoyable. Michelle Limoges, production editor, and Lisa Wehrle, the book's copyeditor, were invaluable with their steady and unfailing attention to all details, big and small. Elizabeth Fogarty's marketing savvy also contributes greatly to this book's success. I also want to thank the reviewers for their patience in reading this text prior to copyediting and for their comments and observations, all of which had a very positive impact on the final version of this work: Lillian McEnery, University of Houston, Clearlake; Michele Southerd, Illinois State University; Carol Wareing, Merrimack College; Elizabeth Witherspoon, Stephen F. Austin State University; and Shelley Xu, California State University, Long Beach.

Beating Them All!
Thirty Days to a Magic Score on
Any Elementary Literacy Instruction
Exam for Teacher Certification

CHAPTER ONE

THE MAGIC SCORE

The preface describes the tests this book covers, the content it addresses, and the method it uses to prepare you for the exam that you face. This chapter explains the exam for which you are preparing in greater detail. First, it discusses the format of your exam, along with important considerations for how its sections are scored. Then, it presents the concept of the magic score—a very important consideration for your preparation for and ultimate success in taking the exam. Finally, this chapter provides an overview of both the content that this text addresses and the remaining chapters of this book.

WHAT TEST FORMATS ARE COVERED?

Exams of literacy instruction vary around the country. Table 1.1 lists the exams and the test formats that this book covers. It shows the location, exam name, and sections for each test. After locating your exam, check its format across each of the columns.

The next two sections explain how exams are scored. If your exam has both written and multiple-choice sections, read both passages. If your exam has only multiple-choice questions, you may skip the first reading. Additional information about your test may also be available at http://ablongman.com/boosalis. After the scoring discussion we present one on magic scores in general and the magic score required for your particular test.

HOW ARE THE ESSAYS SCORED?

Read this section only if your test contains a written section.

The written responses are scored "holistically." This means that two or more trained readers read each response and assign a score to it. Typically, they are trained over a period of days in how to read the essays for content and, yes, grammar. Sample papers (termed *anchors*) are circulated that show students whose papers reflect a score of 4 (the highest award in most cases) and below. At the same time, the raters learn to follow criteria that tell them how to score particular responses and how to reach consensus. What these sessions boil down to is this: If the response has all of the items that the test giver is looking for and the grammar is flawless, it gets a 4. If the essay is deficient in any of these areas, it receives fewer points.

The registration bulletin for your exam explains the rubric that is used to rate your answers, along with the criteria to be applied to them.

Something that you should know before attempting to write an essay that is assessed in this fashion is that, the people who are hired to read your essays eventually grow tired of

TABLE 1.1   Exams and Exam Formats

LOCATION AND EXAM		EXAM FORMAT		
State	*Exam*	*Case Study*	*Essay Responses*	*Multiple Choice*
1. Arizona	AEPA—Elementary (Reading portion)	No	Yes (1)	100
2. California	RICA	Yes	Yes (4)	70
3. California	CSET—MSCP Subtest I: Reading	No	Yes (2)	26
4. Texas	MRTT	Yes	No	100
5. Oklahoma	OPTE/OSAT	No	Yes (3)	Up to 75
6. Massachusetts	MTEL	No	Yes (2)	80+
7. Colorado	PLACE	No	Yes (1)	80+
8. New York	NYSTCE/ATS	No	Yes (1)	80
9. Texas	TExES	No	No	125
	ExCET	No	No	125
10. Michigan	MTTC	No	No	100
11. Illinois	ICTS	No	No	125

evaluating these responses. Reading and scoring fifty or so essays can become really tedious for anyone, so you must assume that they are not giving anyone the benefit of the doubt if information is nonexistent or only referenced in passing. It is extremely important that you write the response in a way that allows the raters to find the information quickly and easily to avoid giving them easy excuses to give you low scores.

You may doubt this information, but past experience has demonstrated its validity. Many students have failed these exams as often as nine times in a row, despite knowing the content well through careful study and experience. But no matter what they tried, they just could not get a passing score on the test. It was only after sitting down and learning how to write the answers to the essay questions exactly as this book describes that they were finally able to pass the exam on their next attempt. While their responses contained exactly the same information as all of the previous attempts, organization and clarity made the difference between what had been failing scores and the ultimate passing score.

Chapter 3 teaches you exactly what to do for all of the essay questions that you may face on the test. It covers cases, lesson plans, procedures, and justifications—the most common question forms that all test takers face.

HOW ARE THE MULTIPLE-CHOICE ITEMS SCORED?

As you might have guessed, you read questions in a booklet and "bubble in" answers on a score sheet with a number 2 pencil. The sheet, in turn, is scored by a machine. No secret there. But here is a bit of information that you may not know: *Not all of your answers may count.* For example, if there are eighty questions, about ten of them are not scored. Those are questions that the test is trying out for inclusion on future exams. There is no way to identify those questions, so you have to do each one as if it is real.

This situation is even more complicated. After carefully reviewing all of the bulletins for the exams, there appears to be no additional weight given to the questions that are counted to make up for the "tryouts." This means that when you take it, you'll actually be *behind* when doing the questions since some of them will be tossed out. Worse, if you're not careful, you might wind up spending thirty minutes on five questions that value absolutely nothing. Wasting time on these exams is a true recipe for failure because you might miss easy questions or scored questions that you can answer in under a minute. As such, the multiple-choice questions themselves require strategies and time management methods that you might never have expected. Fortunately, this book creates effective methods to help you overcome the barriers that all of the multiple-choice sections present. These issues are addressed in Chapter 4.

WHAT'S A MAGIC SCORE?

The magic score is the raw score that you have to keep in mind when you are taking the test. Unfortunately, many of the tests do not include raw scores. Instead of giving a pure number that you have to achieve, they report a scaled score that converts the pure number required to pass to a number from 0–100 or 100–300. You need to know the real number of correct answers that are required to pass. Without that number, it is very difficult to develop a strategic plan.

You need to know the difference between a raw score and a scaled score. If you take a spelling test with ten words, and you spell them all correctly, you get a raw score of 10. A scaled score is different. It calculates where your raw score and the raw scores of a bunch of other students land on the "normal curve." A lot of algebra goes into that calculation to convert your raw score into the scaled score. While the purpose is to allow people to make individual and group comparisons of past and present exam sessions, it does little for you except to hide the exact raw number required to pass the exam. It also prevents other entities from using your scores for something other than teacher certification.

Knowing the raw score for passing really is important. Think of it in this way. If you take a ten-item spelling test and know that you have to get seven correct to pass, *you surely will try to answer seven of those items carefully*! That is the same story with these tests, only you cannot immediately tell how many questions it really takes to pass. Candidates facing the California RICA are fortunate in one way: They know that they have to get a raw score of 81 to pass. That's pretty clear information. The rest of you are not so lucky. All you are given is the scaled score. Estimating the raw score required is extremely important because doing so gives you an idea of how many questions you have to be careful on and how many questions you can skip. This way, you have a better chance at passing the test on your first attempt.

The next section presents the magic score for your test. The number is purposely scaled up to account for questions that are not counted on the exam. The tables that appear in the following sections are meant to help you to understand the magic score that you need to pass the exam and how it is obtained. Knowing this figure will help you to know how many questions you can skip and how many questions you have to answer with great care to increase your chances of passing. Similar tables appear in Chapter 5 and show you how to employ the strategies from Chapters 3 and 4 effectively to earn that magic score.

WHAT'S MY MAGIC SCORE?

Find your test and see for yourself! After locating your exam and reading its description, turn to the overview of the core reading-instruction model that is presented at the end of this chapter. It conveys the content that you have to know for the exam and provides an overview of the information presented in Chapter 2. You may also wish to skim Chapters 3, 4, and 5 to get a sense of the amount of information that you have to learn to achieve that magic score. In addition, it is wise to review the study plan in Chapter 6 carefully so that you can adjust your schedule accordingly.

Arizona Educator Proficiency Assessments (AEPA–Elementary)

The AEPA comes in two varieties: Professional Knowledge and Subject Knowledge. The former assesses a candidate's knowledge of pedagogy, and the latter tests a candidate's knowledge of the subject taught in K–12 education. This preparation book is most useful for preparing for the reading-instruction and reading-content portions of the elementary exam only. Following is the format and magic score for the elementary exam.

Arizona Educator Proficiency Assessments (AEPA)—Elementary Education (Reading)

MAGIC SCORE: 80 POINTS	
■ Essay 1 (300 words)	10 Points
■ Multiple choice (100 items)	70 Points

Source: AEPA Registration Bulletin (2002)

The passing score on the AEPA–Elementary Education is a scaled score of 240 on a 100–300 point scale obtained through an interesting multiplication exercise: Your essay score is multiplied by .1 and your multiple choice score by .9 before they are added and scaled. Any questions?

To simplify things, the magic score to keep in mind is a raw score of 80 from a combined score on both sections. You have four hours to get it. Unfortunately, an unknown number of multiple-choice questions will be thrown out, so Arizona candidates will have to be even more careful when approaching this section. The remaining points will be earned from the essay, where you will hopefully get between 5 and 10 points, after writing about three hundred words. Keeping these numbers in mind will help you reach that magic score of 80, regardless of how many multiple-choice items they intend to throw out. After studying the content of Chapter 2, focus intensely on the essay formats of Chapter 3 and the multiple-choice methods in Chapter 4. You are going to need all the help that you can get for this exam.

California Reading Instruction Competence Assessment (RICA)

MAGIC SCORE: 81 OUT OF 120 POSSIBLE POINTS	
Written portion	**60 points**
Essay 1 (50 words)	6 points
Essay 2 (150 words)	12 points
Essay 3 (150 words)	12 points
Essay 4 (50 words)	6 points
Case study (300 words)	24 points
Multiple choice (70 items)	**60 points**

Source: RICA Registration Bulletin 2002–2003.

The magic score on the RICA is a raw score of 81 out of 120 possible points. You have four hours to get it. Half of the test is written, and it is worth 60 points. The other half is multiple choice, and it is worth 60 points, too. Here is the plan: You need to get at least 50 points out of the written section and at least 41 questions correct on the multiple-choice section. That adds up to an 81. *Not usually,* of course, but remember that ten questions are thrown out, so it is possible to achieve a score of 91 but receive credit for only 81 points in the end.

Here is the structure of the test. The written portion has five parts: one case study of 300 words that is worth 24 points; two short answers of 50 words, each worth 6 points; and two short answers of 150 words that are worth 12 points each. Each is scored by the rubrics described earlier. The multiple-choice section includes 70 questions, but only 60 are scored (no, there is no way to identify those questions).

There are no minimum passing scores on each section of the exam. For example, you can do so-so on the two cheap short answers and still pass. If you do well enough on the writing section but mediocre on the multiple choice, *you're in* if it all adds up to 81 and vice versa. However, if you do poorly on each section and your score adds up to 80 or below, you will have to take (and pay for) the whole test again, regardless of how well you performed on the individual parts of the exam. This can become a very expensive proposition if you don't prepare or if you lack solid content and test strategies. (Don't worry—that's what this book is for.)

California Subject Examinations for Teachers (CSET–MSCP)

The structure of the CSET–MSCP examination includes three subtests over a variety of content areas, 143 multiple-choice items about each content area, and 11 short answers that address each content area. This text is most useful for the reading portion of Subtest 1. Specifically, items 1.3–literacy and 1.4–assessment are addressed in Chapter 2; items 2.3–writing applications, 3.1–concepts and conventions, and 3.3–interpretation of text apply generally.

You will also find the strategies for the essay questions (Chapter 3) and the multiple-choice items (Chapter 4) most useful in your preparation. One important note is that the essay items are very short, so you have to write very focused and tight responses on this exam and its subtest. A separate text entitled, *Beating the CSET!* which addresses the remaining domains and content areas of this test, its magic scores, and time management models may be available soon. For more information, please visit www.ablongman.com.

Texas Master Reading Teacher Test (MRTT)

MAGIC SCORE: 80 POINTS	
Case study (300–600 words)	20 points
Multiple choice (100 items)	80 points

Source: Master Reading Teacher Preparation Manual (2002–2003).

Your magic score is a raw score of 80. A passing score on the MRTT is a scaled score of 240 on a 100–300 point scale. You have five hours to get it. There are both written and multiple-choice sections. Only 80 of your multiple-choice responses count, though. An easier way to look at your magic score is that you have to get 80 points from a combined score on both parts. You can translate the written section to roughly 20 points and the multiple-choice section to about 80 points. The case study is rated on a 4-point scale before your points are awarded. (Caution: you cannot score below a 3 on the case study and still pass this exam!) To obtain a passing raw score on the multiple-choice section alone, you need to be sure on at least 65 questions. This should allow you to get a 15 on the written portion and still pass.

Oklahoma Professional Teaching Examination (OPTE/OSAT) and Oklahoma Subject Area Tests for Teachers (OSAT)

MAGIC SCORE: 80 POINTS	
Written portion	**30 points**
Critical analysis (150 words)	10 points
Student inquiry (150 words)	10 points
Teacher assignment (150 words)	10 points
Multiple choice (Up to 75 items)	**60 points**

Source: OSAT Study Guide, Vol. 1 (2001).

The magic score for this test is 80. A passing score on the OPTE is 240 on a 100–300 point scale. You will have four hours to get it. The exam has two parts, one written section that is worth 30 percent of your score, and a multiple-choice section that is worth 70 percent of your score. We have increased the value of the multiple choice section to account for the unspecified number of items. The written section requires three short answers of about 150 words. Those students facing this exam are advised to read Chapter 3 very carefully. The word counts may vary from section to section, and you need to be prepared for that. The multiple-choice section has up to 75 items depending on whether a written-response question is present. An unknown number of multiple-choice questions will not count. Take the time to verify the number of items with an official test administrator after you've registered for the exam; information on both the *OPTE* and *OSAT* is subject to change. You have to earn at least a 20 on the written portion and a minimum of 60 on the multiple-choice section to earn your magic score of 80. You can do a little worse on the multiple-choice questions if you do really well on the written portion. Since the written portion is much easier to complete than is the multiple-choice section, pay careful attention to the information in Chapter 3, since it explains how to make the most out of the written sections.

Massachusetts Tests for Educator Licensure (MTEL–Reading)

MAGIC SCORE: 80 POINTS	
Written portion	**30 points**
Essay 1 (50–150 words)	15 points
Essay 2 (150–300 words)	15 points
Multiple choice (80 items)	**70 points**

Source: MTEL 2002–2003 Registration Bulletin.

Your magic score is 80. You have four hours to get it. A passing score on the MTEL is a 70 on a 0–100 point scale. There is a written section that is worth approximately 30 percent and a multiple-choice section that weights about 70 percent. The value of the written questions may vary, and though you want to answer all 80 multiple-choice questions, only about 70 count. You need to get at least 20 points on the written portion and 60 on the multiple-choice section. If you do a little better on the written portion, you can do a little worse on the multiple choice. That is not a bad plan since the written questions are easier to complete. Pay careful attention to Chapter 3 because it explains how to make the most out of the written portion of the exam.

Colorado Program for Licensing Assessments for Colorado Educators (PLACE)

MAGIC SCORE: 80 POINTS	
Written portion (300 words)	20 points
Multiple choice (80–100 items)	80 points

Source: PLACE Study Guide, Vol. 2 (2001).

The magic score for this test is approximately 80. A passing score on the Colorado PLACE is 220 on a 100–300 point scale. You have four hours and thirty minutes to get it. To reach the magic score, you should prepare to do really well on the written portion or exceptionally well on the multiple-choice items. The written section is easier to complete, so if you earn 15 points there and at least 65 on the multiple-choice section, a passing score is well within grasp. Read Chapter 3 carefully. It shows you how to write effective essays for this test, and you may just walk out with a perfect score on the written portion.

New York State Teacher Certification
Exam Assessment of Teaching Skills
(NYSTCE/ATS–Written)

MAGIC SCORE: 80 POINTS	
Written portion (300 words)	20 points
Multiple choice (80 items)	80 points

Source: NYSTCE Assessment of Teaching Skills—Written Preparation Guide (2000).

You need to get a magic score of 80. A passing score on the ATS–Written exam is 220 on a 100–300 point scale. You have four hours to get it. The format includes both a written-response and multiple-choice section. The written question is worth about 20 points, and the multiple-choice section is worth 80. Focus your efforts on learning the material in Chapter 3, since the word length looks like that of a case study. Plus, the written section is easier to complete. If you come out of the written portion with at least a 15, you need only a 65 on the multiple-choice section.

Texas Examinations of Educator Standards (TExES)

MAGIC SCORE: 80 POINTS	
Multiple choice (125 items)	100 points

Source: TExES/ExCET Registration Bulletin (2002–2003).

The magic score on this test is approximately 80. The TExES is a five-hour exam with a passing score of 240 on a 100–300 point scale. There are 125 items, but only 100 are scored. Multiple-choice-only exams are no fun. You're going to have to do 90 questions with care since about 25 of them may be tossed out.

Texas Examination for the Certification
of Educators in Texas (ExCET)

MAGIC SCORE: 80 POINTS	
Multiple choice (125 items)	100 points

Source: TExES/ExCET Registration Bulletin (2002–2003).

The magic score on this test is approximately 80. The ExCET is a five-hour exam with a passing score of 70 on a 0–100 point scale. There are 125 items, but only 100 are scored. This means that you have to make good attempts on a minimum of 90 items. Since this test is about to disappear, nothing more needs to be said about it.

Michigan Test for Teacher Certification (MTTC)

MAGIC SCORE: 75 POINTS	
Multiple choice (100 items)	80 points

Source: MTTC Study Guide, Vol. 2 (2001).

The magic score on the exam is approximately 75. You have four hours and thirty minutes to get it. A passing score on the Michigan MTTC is 220 on a 100–300 point scale. The exam includes multiple-choice items only, and 80 items are scored. To get it, you need to be sure on at least 85 of the questions since a number of them may be thrown out. You're going to have to read the content of Chapter 2 carefully. The models in that chapter help you to get through these multiple-choice questions. Also, spend time in Chapter 4, since you are going to need strategies to handle these questions.

Illinois Certification Testing System (ICTS)

MAGIC SCORE: 80 POINTS	
Multiple choice (125 items)	100 points

Source: ICTS Study Guide: Language Arts (1996).

Your magic score is approximately 80. Your passing score on the Illinois ICTS is 70 on a 0–100 point scale. You have five hours to get it. The exam includes 125 multiple-choice items, of which only 100 are scored. To reach your magic score, you need to be sure of your answers on at least 90 of the questions. Chapter 2 offers you models that will help you to survive these questions. Be sure to read it carefully.

WHAT ELSE SHOULD I KNOW?

You should know that information constantly changes on these exams. You are responsible for verifying the information on the passing scores, the formats, the number of written sections, the word counts, and the number of multiple-choice items. The registration bulletins communicate that information to you. Also, after you register, you will be able to ask questions of your test's representative. Take advantage of that. The following are questions that you should be sure to ask to verify the information that you have just read.

- How many sections are there on the test (e.g., written and multiple choice)?
- What percent is assigned to the written portion? The multiple-choice portion?
- What is the point value on each section?
- What raw score must I obtain to pass before it is converted to a scaled score?

- How many multiple-choice questions are there?
- How many are scored?

Getting answers to the above questions will let you know exactly how much margin for error you have on each section of the test. Also, you'll be able to make the best use of the rest of this book. You may also check http://www.ablongman.com/boosalis for any new information about your test.

OVERVIEW OF THE CORE READING-INSTRUCTION MODEL

What follows is an overview of the reading-instruction content that is tested on the exam and a brief explanation of each of its components. After this overview, each of the levels and areas of the model are explained to you fully, so that you will know what you have to know and how you have to know it.

In one shot, Table 1.2 shows the reading-instruction model that you have to know for the test. Brief explanations of each part of this model follow (Ball & Blachman, 1991; Ehri, Nunes, Stahl, & Willows, 2001; Honig, Diamond, Gutlohn, & Mahler, 2000).

TABLE 1.2   Reading-Instruction Model

Level 1: Assessment tools

Individual assessments	Group assessments

Level 2: Decoding (kindergarten through third grade)

Concepts about print	Phonemic awareness	Phonics	Sight words	Spelling

Level 3: Fluency

Choral reading	Repeated reading	Sustained silent reading	At-home reading

Level 4: Comprehension (third grade through eighth grade)

Vocabulary instruction	Literal, inferential, and evaluative comprehension	Pre-, while-, and postreading strategies	Schema strategies

Level 5: Role of oral and written language in literacy instruction

Strategy discussions	Literature circles	Language experience approach	Story frames	Writing process

Level 6: Classroom and unit planning

Selecting texts	Creating centers	Grouping students	Thematic units	Interdisciplinary units

Treat this model of reading instruction as if it has six levels. These levels include assessment, decoding, comprehension, oral and written language development, and classroom planning. Let's walk through each level of the model to get a general idea about what you have to learn for the test.

Level 1: Assessment Principles

The first level of this model is about assessment. Assessment is used to determine who is reading above, at, or below grade level in terms of their reading development within this singular model of reading instruction. Individual and group instruction is then planned accordingly. You learn about major assessments here, particularly those associated with oral reading evaluations. Sections of Chapter 2 discuss specific assessments for areas of the model.

Level 2: Decoding (Learning to Read)

Level 2 is about teaching decoding. You learn all about the expectations for this level of instruction when this level is discussed. For now, be aware of the following ideas. There are five areas of knowledge that you have to know, including *concepts about print, phonemic awareness, phonics, sight words,* and *spelling.* Finally, you are expected to understand how to assess and plan instruction for each of the content areas. Each of these five areas can be viewed as stages of literacy development. For example, children move from concepts about print and phonemic awareness to specific areas of phonics knowledge (Beck & Juel, 1995). Knowing how this process works helps you infinitely on the exam since it enables you to answer questions about what to do with a child who is stuck at some level of concepts about print, in addition to what to do next if the child has mastered concepts about print and phonemic awareness.

Level 3: Fluency

Fluent, accurate decoding is viewed as a gateway that separates instructing students in automatic decoding from teaching students how to comprehend what they read independently (Kibby, 1989). Central to this notion is attention: If students cannot decode text fluently, without halting and stumbling over the words they decode in print, their attention will be on making and correcting errors and not on understanding. Put simply, there may not be enough attention left over to understand what is being read if major decoding problems are present in the students' oral reading. There are both teacher-directed and independent ways to help students develop fluency, and for the test you need to learn how these strategies are used.

Level 4: Comprehension (Reading to Learn)

Level 4 is about reading comprehension. There are several major areas here. The first area is vocabulary development. Vocabulary development is beyond the basic level and refers to words that may not be part of the child's spoken vocabulary: The higher the level of text, the more complex the vocabulary becomes. The simple decoding strategies that you learn about in Level 2 may not work for these types of words; instead, children need additional strategies to *comprehend* these words. For example, a fourth grader might be able to decode the word *antidisestablishmentarianism,* but not understand it. In the upper-elementary grades, the children have to learn advanced strategies for unlocking the meanings of complex words like this one.

The next components at this level include comprehension levels, reading strategies, and text schema. There are three types of comprehension that you have to know well, along with the activities that go along with their development. *Literal, inferential,* and *evaluative comprehension* are the terms you have to get to know. Literal comprehension refers to understanding what is read in a factual way. Children who have literal comprehension can answer simple, factual questions about who, what, where, and when things happen in a story. Inferential comprehension builds on literal comprehension to look at how and why things happen. Evaluative comprehension makes objective and subjective assessments of what one is reading both personally and in relation to other works. Strategies exist to increase comprehension at each of the three levels. The type of text, too, affects the instructional activities that one selects to develop reading comprehension. You have to know all of these for the test.

Each of the components at this level of the model work together: As vocabulary develops, comprehension increases. Furthermore, as literal comprehension increases, so does inferential comprehension. The teacher plays a direct role in ensuring that each of these areas increases to its fullest potential for students. As such, you have to know specific types of activities that help students to grow in each of the areas of Level 4.

Level 5: Oral and Written Language Development

Level 5 is about oral and written language development. It spans kindergarten through the upper grades. After you learn about how this model views decoding, fluency, and comprehension, your next step is to understand the ways that oral and written language figure into supporting reading instruction for emergent and proficient readers.

Level 6: Classroom Planning

It might seem strange to see that classroom planning is discussed last, rather than right at the beginning. But in this model, classroom planning is built around assessment results and the areas of the model in which the students are working. In kindergarten through third grade, classroom planning is based around assessments and instruction for decoding. That means that the types of books that you select for the classroom are related to decoding; the activities that you conduct are related to decoding; and the ways that you group students are related to needs in decoding.

Upper-elementary classrooms, in contrast, are constructed around assessments and activities to develop comprehension. Again, this affects the types of books used in the classroom, the writing activities, and so forth. You have to consider the types of text that should be used, how to make them engaging and accessible, and how to plan units of study. Assessment results and grade-level expectations, then, affect how you do all of your unit planning, student grouping, and instruction. "Correct" answers on the test depend on your knowledge of how this system of planning and assessment works.

Summary of the Core Reading-Instruction Model

Please note that the descriptions here are brief and refer only to the reading-instruction model that you need to learn. The information is restricted to this model and is not meant to be sufficient for separate exams of content and instruction for English as a second language or special education students. However, the information is sufficient for adapting reading instruction related to this model.

Each of the areas of this comprehensive model work together to articulate a picture of literacy instruction in kindergarten through eighth grade. First, you learn how assessment and planning occur in these grades. Second, you learn how to teach decoding to students who are not yet reading. Third, you see how to help them to decode fluently. Fourth, you learn how to develop reading comprehension. Then, you learn about the roles that oral and written language development play in literacy instruction. Finally, you learn how to plan the classroom accordingly. As you read and study, keep this model in mind.

CONCLUSION

The remaining chapters of this book teach you the content, written and multiple-choice strategies, and time management methods that you need to know for your test. The last chapter shows you how to put all of this information together through a thirty-day study plan so that you can get the exam behind you as quickly as possible. Also visit http://www.ablongman.com/boosalis for the latest information on your test and other sources that are valuable supplements to your preparation.

CHAPTER TWO

MAGIC CONTENT

The information presented in this chapter is essential. The way that the content is laid out will make the process of learning it quite easy. Tables summarize the information in a particular area for you first, and then the principles, assessments, and activities that exemplify that area of study are given. This way, you are able to see the concepts visually before they are described to you. It will also be very helpful for you to refer to the summary model presented in Chapter 1 from time to time. Doing so will keep you focused on how much progress you are making through the material, and you will be able to maintain a view of the "big picture," too.

A NOTE ABOUT TESTS WITH WRITTEN PORTIONS

All of the assessments and activities in this chapter are written in a way that makes the transition to essay writing an easy one. Each activity is constructed to convey the steps, materials, and ideas that you must include to increase your chances of receiving a better-than-average score on the written portion of the test. Obviously, it is important for you to practice writing out each of the activities in this chapter, along with the summary tables, so that the essays flow from your pen with ease.

A NOTE ABOUT TESTS WITH
MULTIPLE-CHOICE SECTIONS

The content of Chapter 2 and its presentation will help you immensely on the multiple-choice portion of the exam. Many of the questions ask you about what to do "first" and "next" with a child who has a particular need in some area of the model. Take phonemic awareness, for example.

A kindergarten teacher wishes to assess her students' knowledge of phonemic awareness. Which of the following items best describes the first ability that the teacher should assess?

A. Segmenting spoken words into individual sounds
B. Blending individual sounds into spoken words
C. Identifying initial sounds in matching spoken words
D. Identifying initial sounds in spoken words

The only way to know that the correct answer is D is to understand not only the content, but also the fixed order of assessment. This idea holds true for all areas of the core content model. You should write out the tables presented in Appendix A and answer the questions in Chapter 6 to learn the content effectively.

HOW WAS THE CONTENT DEVELOPED?

Reviews of the reading-instruction content stated in all of the available registration bulletins produced an easy-to-understand model. This text takes that model and analyzes the subsections within it to ensure that the material is covered the way it "ought" to be covered—that is, that the content aligns with what is on the test. To make studying for the content easier, the text also uses tables to summarize what you need to know within each section. The tables also make the information clear and easy to learn.

THE CORE MODEL OF READING INSTRUCTION EXPLAINED

In the next sections, the core model of reading instruction that is introduced in Chapter 1 is explained to you. You will learn the content, assessments, and activities that are tested most often on these exams. Since you may need to refer to the overview table from Chapter 1 often, mark that page so that you can locate it with ease.

LEVEL 1: ASSESSMENT TOOLS

Assessment in this model is used to figure out which students are reading above, at, or below grade level so that you can plan instruction according to their needs. For you to understand what these literacy assessments are supposed to indicate, you have to know something about the expectations that occur at each grade level. The easiest distinction to grasp is the one that divides "learning-to-read" and "reading-to-learn" (O'Mally, 1998).

Ideally, "learning-to-read" occurs in kindergarten through third grade. Here, children learn the foundations of decoding (concepts about print and phonemic awareness), decoding skills (phonics), and rapid, automatic decoding of text (fluency). Heavy emphasis is on skills instruction, particularly in the areas of learning to decode print and the foundations that precede that ability. By grade 3, all of these areas must be in place. Specific assessments determine how well students are doing in the learning-to-read process so that you can plan instruction for those who are above, at, or below their peers. You learn about the assessments and expectations for these areas when we discuss decoding (Level 2) and fluency (Level 3).

Comprehension is deemphasized during learning-to-read activities because this model is very strict about how children learn to decode. During decoding instruction, comprehension is seen as a hindrance because it takes attention away from the print that the child is "learning-to-read." Please note that comprehension is taught to students who are learning to read, but instruction occurs separately and usually in the form of oral retellings, oral questions, drawings, or other forms of expressions that do not rely on print.

"Reading-to-learn" occurs in grades 4 and above in this ideal world. Here, students learn how to gain knowledge independently from a variety of narrative and informational and scientific texts. This means that they need instruction in strategies that allow them to work with text independently and to demonstrate that they have understood what they have read, regardless of whether the text is a short story or an article on gene therapy. Assessments show where students are having difficulty comprehending a variety of narrative and informational texts, and the results impact how you teach students who are above, at, or below meeting these expectations. The discussion of comprehension (Level 4) presents the assessments and expectations for reading to literacy.

We next guide you through the first level of the model. It discusses assessments in reading instruction, which include informal reading inventories, running records, miscue analyses, portfolio assessments, and group assessments. This discussion will help your performance on questions related to data analysis and to assessing a child's reading development.

There is a wide variety of assessments in reading instruction that you have probably experienced already. For your exam, however, it is essential that you know the assessments presented next, particularly the ones that gauge a child's independent reading level, reading processes, and individual and group progress. Other assessment tools are described within the remaining levels of the model, but for now the text deals only with the most common assessment tools available.

The items below capture the assessments for individual and groups of students.

INDIVIDUAL ASSESSMENTS
- Informal reading inventories
- Running records
- Miscue analyses
- Portfolios

GROUP ASSESSMENTS
- Norm-referenced tests
- Criterion-referenced tests

The first important distinction that you need to make is between individual and group assessments of reading. No further elaboration should be necessary. The second distinction, however, needs some explanation. There is an important difference between process and product assessments. Process assessments look at both the strategies that a student uses to arrive at a correct or incorrect response and the skills that he either displays or neglects when reading aloud. These highly individualized assessments, for example, reveal how one student uses the first letters to decode words, while another student uses an entirely different process for decoding the same print. These individualized assessments allow for individualized instruction: instruction that is tailored to the specific needs of a particular student.

Product assessments, on the other hand, look only at quantifiable outcomes, such as the number correct on a spelling test. Standardized assessments of reading are the most obvious (and largest) form of product assessment available. These tests allow one to compare an individual student's score with other members of the same group or, even more broadly, an entire classroom's score with the scores from other classrooms within the school, the district, the state, the country, or the world. As you see later in the chapter, their view is very different from the individual process assessments that you learn about next.

Individual Assessments

Individual assessments of reading look at how a particular child uses or neglects skills and strategies in her reading. As their name implies, individual assessments test individual children to see what they do as they read text aloud. For example, does the child look at the print when reading? Is the child neglecting certain strategies or skills when reading? Individual assessments tell you very specific things about what a child needs to be taught to become a successful reader.

The type of individual process assessment that you need to know best is the one that helps you to determine a student's independent reading level. These assessments include informal reading inventories, miscue analyses, and running records. They can be given on the spot and tell a teacher what a child can do right now. After the discussion of informal reading inventories, miscue analyses, and running records, you learn about a broad type of process assessment available. This is called portfolio assessment, and it provides a picture of a child's reading development over a period of days, weeks, months, or even years.

Informal Reading Inventories.   Informal reading inventories (IRIs) test grade-level passages from which children read aloud. The grade levels are determined in a variety of ways, including the frequency of the words as they occur in children's literature for a particular age, the complexity of the letter combinations of each word, or the number of syllables each word contains. In this model, because decoding is such an important part of its design, passages with regular and irregular phonetic (for example, letter patterns) are most likely to appear on the exam.

As the child reads a given IRI passage aloud, the teacher scores the child's performance on her copy of the same passage using a standard set of symbols. These symbols are then analyzed separately to develop a picture of what skills the child displays or neglects when decoding print. Instruction is then planned accordingly. In short, answering questions about IRIs and what they tell you is an important part of the exam. The questions range from your having to explain or demonstrate that you know how to administer assessments properly, or interpreting assessment data by answering a series of questions or written-response tasks that ask you to remediate an appropriate skill or strategy for instruction.

Understanding the following key ideas will prepare you to answer questions about IRIs, including how IRIs are administered, scored, and interpreted.

Administering IRIs.   A common way to administer an IRI is through student oral recitation. The teacher provides no assistance to the student during the reading. The primary purpose of the IRI is to determine a child's independent reading level and to reveal the processes that the student uses or neglects when decoding print, not to measure the teacher's ability to intervene. Determining an independent reading level is important because it tells the teacher the books that should be used during independent reading time during class or sent home to be read with the family. Reading levels also indicate which books should be used with the children during one-on-one or small-group instruction and which books should be withheld for a while.

IRIs also tell teachers about the reading processes that students do and do not use when decoding print. This forms part of the basis for instruction since a teacher's planning is based on the student's or a group of students' strengths and needs. Strengths and needs are determined through postanalyses of what the child does when reading aloud. For example, the child may appeal to the teacher for help, repeat certain words, mispronounce others, and self-correct errors. Each of these behaviors informs the teacher about how to target instruction. Miscue analyses, discussed later, are more in-depth analyses that occur after the IRI and provide teachers with even more information about planning instruction.

Here is how IRIs are used in classes. Imagine that you have twenty first graders who enter your class at the beginning of the year. What you do is assess each child individually in a quiet area of the classroom to determine a reading level and identify relative strength and needs. This helps you to plan instruction. Many IRIs come prepackaged with a word list, numbered passages, and books that correspond to those numbered passages, and you start with the word list.

Word List.   Typically, a list of words with regular and irregular phonetic patterns is used as the initial assessment in this model. There are other entry points available, but individual words are most common here. So, when assessing all twenty children, you might begin with a word list. The words lists tell you which passage to begin with to determine the independent reading level. The words are grouped into words that kindergarteners, first graders, second graders, and so on should be able to decode. The words increase in complexity as the grade levels increase, moving from simple words such as *cat* to more complex words with lots of letter combinations and syllables, such as *extremely.*

The child reads the words aloud from his copy of the list, while the teacher marks the child's rendition on her copy of the same list. Table 2.1 shows an example. During this initial assessment, the teacher does not intervene. As you can see in Table 2.1, the student decoded the first word correctly, the second word incorrectly (using a interesting letter-decoding strategy), the third word incorrectly (supplying an incorrect word), and the fourth word by skipping it entirely. The standard cut off for a grade-level reading is 80 percent.

TABLE 2.1   Word List

	LEVEL 2 WORDS	CHILD'S RESPONSE
1.	*cat*	correct
2.	*the*	t-he
3.	*ran*	run
4.	*Sam*	—

Once the child misses more than 20 percent of the words on a particular list, you turn to the reading passages and start a level or two below the highest level that the child could read. For example, if a fifth grader reads words from the fourth-grade list proficiently, you start at a second- or third-grade level. Doing so provides the child with the opportunity to warm up and build confidence, as one does with physical exercise.

Reading Passages. After administering the word list, you then have the child begin with the reading passages. As the child reads aloud, you mark all of the behaviors that she exhibits during the reading. The behaviors include words that the child skips over, inserts improperly, substitutes, mispronounces, or that the teacher has to supply for the student. Figure 2.1 shows the typical symbols used for scoring (Clay, 1993a; Gunning, 2003; Vacca et al., 2003). Remember that the purpose of these assessments is to determine both the student's independent reading level and what areas of decoding need attention. These errors tell you where to begin instruction for the student. The following formula and the corresponding percentages are generally accepted for calculating the student's independent, instructional, and frustration reading levels (Clay, 1993a). The formula is simple: You take the total number of words read minus the errors and divide that by the total number of words read. For example, if the child read 100 words with 5 errors, you divide 95 by 100. This gives you 95, or 95 percent. The percentages tell you the student's reading level.

INDEPENDENT: 96 PERCENT AND ABOVE
- Books at this level are appropriate for independent and at-home reading.

INSTRUCTIONAL: 95–90 PERCENT
- Books at this level are the ones used for one-on-one or small-group instruction when the students have similar needs.

FRUSTRATION: 89 PERCENT AND BELOW
- Books at this level are withheld until the child's instructional reading level rises.

Remember that IRIs typically come with a series of books that corresponds to the passages, so that if a child is reading independently on a "series" three on the passages, the books from this series that are sent home with the child and used during sustained silent reading in class. Similarly, the teacher selects books for one-on-one instruction from the series that corresponds to the instructional reading level. Books that are in the series that represent the student's frustration level are not used since they are too difficult for now.

$\frac{dog}{dig}$ Substitution   ☐ Deletion

∧ Insertion   ⟵ Repetitions

© Self-correction | Pause   **FIGURE 2.1   Oral Reading Symbols**

You can envision the philosophy of assessment and instruction in this model in the following way:

> Today's instructional level books are tomorrow's independent level books; today's frustration level books are tomorrow's instructional level books.

The teacher's task is to plan instruction based on assessment to make the above possible.

Comprehension Questions and IRIs.   You may see comprehension questions after the scored IRI passages on the test. These questions are typically printed at the bottom of each passage, and the child supplies answers to them by either having them read to her or by reading and answering them independently. In either case, the teacher usually allows the child to read the passage again, but silently this time. The reason that a second, silent reading is advised has to do with performance: When children read aloud, they often focus their attention on "doing it right" rather than on understanding the text. As such, the second chance allows the child time to focus entirely on comprehension.

The types of comprehension questions that teachers ask students after the IRI passage fall into two categories: literal and inferential. A full explanation of both types of comprehension questions and their levels appears later in this chapter (see Level 4: Comprehension). For now, the following definitions are sufficient.

- Literal comprehension questions reveal whether the child has understood the factual information in the passage. These questions ask *who, what, where,* and *when* questions about characters in stories, plots, and events, and are the most basic level of question that one can ask.
- Inferential questions reveal whether the child can read "beyond" the text, using his factual understandings as a point of departure. *How* and *why* questions are examples. For example, questions such as *How did the character feel?* and *Why is the character pretending to be happy?* require the student to base responses on many elements of the story. Because of all of the comprehension demands, inferential questions are thought to be at a higher level than literal questions are.

As the child provides answers to these two types of questions, the teacher may make other observations, too. Recording whether the student's responses are recalled freely or with teacher prompting is a part of the assessment process. In addition, some IRIs are used to gauge listening comprehension, so be sure to look at any available notes carefully since you may write an excellent essay or select answers about a student's "excellent" reading skills when the child has actually not read anything at all.

It is also possible that you will see no comprehension questions at all after analyzing IRI data. Remember that this model is very focused on decoding; as such, there may be no comprehension questions available for you to analyze.

Initial and In-depth IRI Analyses.   When you take the test, you may see questions that require you to make very quick analyses of IRI data or data taken from what is termed a *mis-*

cue analysis. Data are analyzed for you so that you can quickly identify correct answers to questions that use IRI data. It is also helpful if you remember that you are going to validate "test reality"—not "real reality"—when you take the exam.

A simple glance at the IRI data tells you how much progress the child is making when reading, if you keep the following information in mind. There is a hierarchy to consider: Some types of errors show more progress than others do. For example, high numbers of omissions, in which the student skips a word that she does not know, show very little progress because the child is not using any strategies to decode the print. Figure 2.2 shows an example. The high number of omissions indicates that the child uses neither decoding skills nor initial letter strategies when attempting to decode words as seen in this sentence of regularly patterned, decodable words. Instruction would then focus on acquiring and learning effective strategies to decode these words independently.

The data set in Figure 2.3 shows emerging decoding skills and an initial sound-letter decoding strategy. Compare the data set in Figure 2.3 with the one in Figure 2.2. The high number of initial letter attempts and substitutions reflect that the student has emerging decoding skills on which to build fluent decoding. Decoding words by initial sound is important because the strategy shows that the child is attending to print. Substituting words (for example, *man* for *mat* and *ham* for *hat*) is also an indication that the student is trying to decode the words using a strategy that has some relationship to the print. Instruction would focus on learning how to decode the letters and their combinations within the words (see Level 2: Decoding later in this chapter).

Errors with sight words may also be present in the IRI data on the test. *Sight words* are words that occur frequently in print but are difficult to decode using the usual phonics strategies and rules. For example, the words, *where* and *there* should be read as *weer* and *theer* since the silent *e* at the end of the word should make the vowel in the middle say its name. Words such as *the, then, there, here,* and *where* are common sight words that the child must know from memory.

The data in Figure 2.4 show that the child substitutes one sight word with another sight word that looks similar. A high number of errors with sight words demonstrates a need in this area of instruction. A full discussion of sight word activities takes place when decoding instruction is addressed (Level 3, later in this chapter).

The cat sat on the mat. He saw a rat near a hat.   **FIGURE 2.2 High Number of Omissions**

t... can s...   t... man   s...   r   ham   **FIGURE 2.3 Initial Sound Decoding/**
The cat sat on the mat. He saw a rat near a hat.   **Substituting**

here saw   where
Where was the cat? There is the cat!   **FIGURE 2.4 Sight Word Errors**

FIGURE 2.5   Insertions

$$\overset{\text{big}}{\text{The} \wedge \text{cat sat on the} \wedge \text{mat. He saw a} \wedge \text{rat near a} \wedge \text{hat.}}$$

big   red   big   blue
The ^cat sat on the ^mat. He saw a ^rat near a ^hat.

Another error variety is the insertion, shown in Figure 2.5. It occurs when a child inserts a word in the text where there is no print. Insertions show that the child is relying on something other than the print while decoding. The amount of progress that these errors show is negligible, according to this model, because the mistakes still demonstrate that the child is not relying on print when reading, regardless of how much "meaning" the child is making from the text. Furthermore, the "danger" is that the child may develop a habit of inserting words into the text that might not be a hindrance at this level of print, but may become one later on in development.

Having described a simple hierarchy of errors that you can use to analyze data quickly on the exam, we now turn to self-corrections. Self-corrections occur when the child reads decodable print, makes an error, and then repairs the mistake independently. Figure 2.6 shows an example of self-corrections. In the real world, high numbers of self-corrections may be a very good sign. Even though the child is still struggling to decode print, at least she is trying to use strategies to repair errors in reading. But in this model, self-corrections are still a problem.

The next discussion presents running records before discussing self-correction in-depth. Running records are similar to IRIs in terms of their scoring; however, they are far more flexible than the assessments just described.

Running Records.   Running records share something in common with IRIs: Teachers use them to determine independent reading levels and to reveal the processes that students use when reading text aloud. When taking a running record, teachers use the same symbols to document omissions, substitutions, and insertions. However, running records are far more flexible than IRIs are. Teachers mark the student's performance on a blank recording sheet, rather than on a prefabricated text sheet. This enables a teacher to perform running record analyses on any text that the child happens to be reading. For example, the running record can be taken during sustained silent reading when all of the children are reading a variety of texts. Here, the teacher can approach the child, ask the student to read aloud briefly, and mark the rendition on a blank piece of paper. Figure 2.7 is a hypothetical example of a reading of the following sentences: *The cat sat on the mat near a hat.* The check

FIGURE 2.6   High Number of Self-Corrections

that© saw©   was©   ham©
The cat sat on the mat. He saw a rat near a hat.

✓ ✓ $\frac{\text{saw}}{\text{sat}}$ ✓ ✓ ✓

FIGURE 2.7   Running Record   ✓ ✓ ✓ ✓ ✓

marks indicate the words that the child read correctly from the sentences. The error is captured by writing what the child read (*saw*) above how the text actually read (*sat*). Flexibility, then, is the major distinguishing characteristic that you should know if you are asked to differentiate running records from informal reading inventories.

Next is a discussion of miscue analyses, a postanalysis of either IRI or running record data with errors and self-correction.

Miscue Analyses.   Teachers conduct miscue analyses after carrying out IRIs or running records. The analyses looks at two things: the errors and the self-corrections. Errors and self-corrections indicate the processes that the student uses while reading to make and correct mistakes. The processes are called cueing systems, and there are three of them (Goodman, 1996):

- Meaning/semantics (e.g., reading with the meaning in mind)
- Visual/graphophonics (e.g., reading with the print in mind)
- Syntax/grammar (e.g., reading with the grammar in mind)

When a child makes and self-corrects errors, you can recognize the processes that the child uses or neglects when reading. For example, if the child reads *dog* each time the word *canine* appears, she might be relying on meaning (or the picture that is above the text) rather than on pure print (visual) information. The visual cueing system is also apparent in what substitutions a child makes. Substitutions may indicate that the child is looking only at the print and not thinking about what he is reading. For example, if the child substitutes the word *cat* for any three-letter word that starts with the letter *c* such as *car, can,* or *cap,* the child is not thinking much about the meaning of the sentence. Finally, the syntactic cueing system is most apparent when the child attempts to make book language sound like regular speech. For example, if the text asks, *Where are those two going?,* and the child reads, *Where are they going?,* the child might be trying to simplify the grammar present in the text.

There are other common examples of each of these cueing systems that you need to know for the test. Both examples used here walk through two separate analyses of error and self-corrections and use the data set in Figure 2.8. The title of the book is *The Cat,* and the text reads: *The cat sat on the mat.* Above the text is a picture of a cat sitting on a blue mat. The data in Figure 2.8 show errors and self-corrections. First, analyze the self-corrections. The child has skipped the word *the,* substituted *can* for *cat,* and *Sam* for *sat,* skipped *the* again, inserted the word *blue,* and substituted *man* for *mat.* Table 2.2 shows a miscue analysis of the errors. What was written in the text appears in the "Text" column, while what the child supplied while reading the text aloud appears in the "Child" column. The cueing systems at work for each error are noted in the "Meaning," "Syntax," and "Visual" columns with a check mark.

FIGURE 2.8   Error Data

TABLE 2.2 Miscue Analysis of Errors

	TEXT	CHILD	MEANING	SYNTAX	VISUAL
1.	the	—			
2.	cat	can		✔	✔
3.	sat	Sam			✔
4.	the	th…			✔
5.	—	blue	✔	✔	
6.	mat	man		✔	✔

Let's look at each error more closely.

1. The child skipped the word *the*. No cueing system was at work.
2. The child substituted the word *can* for *cat*. The visual column is checked because there is a relationship between the way *cat* is written and the way *can* is written. The words share two letters in common.
3. The child substituted *Sam* for *sat*. The visual column is checked because *Sam* and *sat* share two letters in common.
4. The child said the initial sound in the word *the* in an attempt to decode it. Because the child attempted to decode the word using a part of the word, the visual column is checked.
5. The child inserted the word *blue* into the text. The meaning and syntax columns are checked because the child might have inserted the word based on the information shown in the picture above the text. The syntax column is also checked because the insertion makes grammatical sense.
6. The child substituted the word *man* for *mat*. Since the words share common letters, a check appears in the visual column.

What this miscue analysis tells you about the child's errors is that she relieves relies heavily on visual information when reading. At times, the child does read for meaning and for grammar, but the predominant cueing system at work is the visual (print) system. This helps the teacher to plan instruction in either skills or strategies (which is discussed later in this section).

Miscue analyses of self-correction data also occur after analyzing any errors that are present. They tell you about the processes at work when children repair the miscues they make when reading. Table 2.3 shows an example and an analysis. The child is accessing a number of cueing systems to self-correct the errors she made initially. A miscue analysis of these errors helps you know what systems she uses when repairing the mistakes. Here is what this analysis tells you.

1. The child self-corrected her substitution of *can* for *cat*. The drastic difference in meaning between *can* and *cat* may have caused the child to look more carefully at the visual (print) to repair the error. Checks appear in both the meaning and visual columns.

TABLE 2.3 **Secondary Analysis of Self-Corrections**

	ERROR	SELF-CORRECTION	MEANING	SYNTAX	VISUAL
1.	can	cat	✔		✔
2.	Sam	sat	✔	✔	✔

2. The child self-corrected her substitution of *Sam* for *sat.* The child may have asked herself if the phrase *the cat Sam,* made sense meaningfully (Does that make sense?) and grammatically (Do we say phrases like that?). Since what the child read made neither meaningful nor grammatical sense, she may have gone back, checked the print, and changed her decoding to the correct word, *sat.* Checks appear in all columns for meaning, syntax, and visual cues.

These self-corrections reveal progress because the student can both decode and repair errors as she reads. Again, initial instruction is in teaching the child to decode words based solely on their letters, letter patterns, or other print features; however, later stages of development ask the child to learn how to use strategies to self-correct errors for words that they are fully capable of decoding.

Skills or Strategies Instruction? It is important to note that this model tends to prescribe skills instruction during the learning-to-read stage and reserves strategies instruction for children who are at the reading-to-learn stage and are learning how to comprehend what they read. This is because the model tends to view all children's miscues, *even their self-corrections,* as hindrances to learning to decode. Decoding instruction, as in Level 2 of this model, describes skills-based instruction (for example, drills, exercises, and direct teacher interventions). As such, select answers on the test that prescribe skills instruction for children who show high numbers of decoding errors, regardless of whether the errors correspond to the meaning, syntax, or visual cueing systems.

In case you are asked questions about decoding strategies instruction, here are some suggestions. Decoding strategies instruction begins after the children demonstrate that they possess solidifying decoding skills. It teaches them tactics to self-correct their mistakes as they read. The following are typical types of self-questions that may help students to self-monitor and regulate their reading on the way toward independence (Kinnucan-Welch, Magill, & Dean, 1999).

Meaning	I read _____.	Does that make sense?
Syntax	I read _____.	Do we say that?
Visual	I read _____.	Does that look right?

If the test data show the child's self-correcting abilities are emerging, these strategies might be viable options on the exam. However, you are probably on safer ground to stick with skills-based decoding instruction to remedy all needs related to decoding print, re-gardless of whether the child self-corrects.

Portfolio Assessments.   In contrast to the narrow individual assessments, portfolios take a very long view of a child's literacy development: They are collections of artifacts that reflect a child's ability to read and write. The items are taken from as many sources as possible so that the portfolio shows a complete and authentic picture of a student's abilities (Courtney & Abodeeb, 1999). This way, a teacher has a complete and "contextualized" view of who the child is, what she can do, and where her needs are. Two portfolio sections that are important for you to know about for the test are described next. They document reading and writing for teacher/student conferences (Mitchell, Abernathy, & Gowans, 1998).

Reading Sections.   Portfolios can include all of the child's IRIs, word lists, miscue analy-ses, and running records so that you and the child can see the progress made over the year. These documents also illustrate areas of continuing need that you and the child still must ad-dress. Reading lists, too, are important. They show the numbers of books, the books' genres, magazines, and other types of literature that the student is reading inside and outside class. This helps both the student and the teacher see progress in the kind and quality of books that the child selects (or avoids) for reading. In short, this section should reflect a total picture of the child's reading ability from the beginning of the year to the present moment.

Writing Section.   The writing section collects all of the pieces of writing that the child cre-ates, errors and all. These artifacts can be drafts of poems, complete poems, informal notes, letters to characters from stories, and so on. They also document all of the work that goes into a paper that the child has written for research projects. This means that all of the pre-writing, the inspirations for writing (including pictures, graphics, and the like), and early notes are part of this section. Drafts and revisions are also made part of this section, along with comments from the teacher and peers regarding the strengths and needs of the writing. All of these items are important because they help the teacher and the child see all of the work that went into writing a research paper. Instead of looking only at the final product and assigning a grade to it, portfolios give a comprehensive view of a child's development. If you have ever felt that a final number on a test or a letter grade was an inadequate means of assessing the real amount of work that went into something that you've done, then you can appreciate the purpose of the portfolio's long view of student development.

Conferences.   Conferences with the child about the portfolio are essential. During these conferences, the teacher and the student discuss the progress that the child has made, along with areas of continuing need. For example, the reading section might show that the child reads a great deal of simple narratives but few expository pieces from journals. The teacher and the student can set goals together to improve this area of the portfolio. Similarly, the writing section reveals to both the teacher and the student where the child's strengths and needs lie. For example, the writing might reflect strong organization and a high level of in-terest, but weak style. The teacher and the student can discuss this need and make plans for how the student can improve this area of the writing. Subsequent conferences would look at progress in these areas, as well as new ones, as they arise.

Other Portfolio Sections. The remaining two of the four skills, speaking and ~~writing,~~ *listening* can also be included in portfolios. Audio and video records, for example, of public speaking are artifacts that one could collect, along with assessment records of listening comprehension. Later in this chapter, you learn about reading-response journals and learning logs (see Level 4: Comprehension). These types of journals can be included as part of the portfolio, too.

Evaluation. Two types of evaluation take place when portfolios are used: student self-assessment and teacher assessment. In a student self-assessment, the child reflects on specific areas of the portfolio and on the strengths and needs that he can see in the work (Bottomley, Henk, & Melnick, 1997/1998). The reflections might address whether the student is meeting or has met any stated goals, recognizes his own strengths and needs, and whether any new goals need to be set or old goals need to be revised. This helps the child to develop a sense of inner control and self-direction to set goals and make plans to meet them (Serafini, 2000/2001). This is a highly personal approach that differs drastically from standardized testing that shows a child's progress at only one moment in time (see Product Assessments).

Teachers also evaluate portfolios. Rubric assessments are the most common assessment tool (Farr & Tone, 1998). Rubrics award points based on whether the child has met a stated goal. These goals, called criteria, can be set by the school, by the teacher, or through discussions with the class or an individual student. The section Criterion-Referenced Assessments in this chapter provides more information on the subject. The following is a brief example.

POINTS	CRITERIA
3 points	Has met the criteria for punctuating declarative sentences
2 points	Has nearly met the criteria for punctuating declarative sentences
1 point	Has not met the criteria for punctuating declarative sentences

The criteria for punctuating declarative sentences, in this case, is set for and made clear to the student, perhaps by being posted in the front of the class or at the writing center. In addition, this expectation is taught prior to assessment and maybe even agreed on by class consensus, depending on how the rubric is designed. The teacher reviews the portfolio and awards points based on the evidence of having met, nearly met, or not met the goal. Points from other sections are then summed and weighed against a scale to assign a grade. A number of conferences take place prior to the final grade, so that the child has multiple opportunities to meet the criteria.

We will now move away from individual assessments to group assessments. You will learn about norm-referenced and criterion-referenced tests next.

Group Assessments

The group product assessments that you need to understand include norm- and criterion-referenced tests. You need to know how they differ and what the results of each type of assessment tell you. Keep in mind that the purpose of your studies here is to prepare for potential multiple-choice and written-response questions that may ask you for specific information about assessments in general or to judge the relative value of a given assessment tool or plan.

Norm-Referenced Tests.   For the test, you need to have some basic understandings of norm-referenced tests. For example, you could be asked to communicate the results of the test to caregivers about their children's performance on an assessment. Or you might have to select correct multiple-choice items about why a particular assessment tool fails in its purpose or design. Knowing how these assessments are carried out and why they are used could be crucial for earning points toward your magic score.

You have to learn three terms that apply to norm-referenced testing: *reliability, validity,* and *reporting.* Reporting has other terms associated with it, including *raw score, rank,* and *grade-equivalent score.* Here is an illustration of the terms in context.

Suppose that you want to know how well fourth-grade students spell the months of the year. You would first have to ask every fourth-grade teacher in the country to administer an assessment to their students, tally the scores, and send the results in to a central location. That central location would then crunch the numbers and tell you how well fourth graders around the country spell the months of the year. For such a scheme to work, you would have to have a spelling test that is *valid* and *reliable.* Here is what *valid* and *reliable* mean in context. Imagine two teachers, Ms. Peterson in Richfield, Minnesota, and Mr. Johnson in Provo, Utah. Both teachers are asked to develop tests that accurately measure spelling, and only spelling, over and over again. Let's look at some issues in reliability and validity using Ms. Peterson and Mr. Johnson as examples, so that you can pick out correct answers about reliability and validity.

If Ms. Peterson gives an oral exam to her students, who then recite the spellings individually, while Mr. Johnson administers a multiple-choice test in which the students pick the correct spelling of each month of the year, they are going to wind up with data that are wholly unreliable and invalid. Ms. Peterson's problem is with reliability. Reliability means that the test measures things the same way every time it is used. Ms. Peterson's approach of having the children spell the words aloud after she says them may yield different results for each child. For example, having each child spell the word *December* orally gives clues to some of students who are listening and confuses others. Each child who spells the word *December* in front of the group muddies the conditions just a bit more for the other children. Worse, if other teachers adopt this same assessment approach, all of the conditions may vary. In short, the spelling scores are faulty since the conditions change for each child who spells the words.

Mr. Johnson's problem is with validity. Validity is the idea that the test measures what it says it measures. Since we are trying to figure out whether the children can spell the months of the year correctly, we have to be sure that we are using a test that will do that and not something else. You can argue that Mr. Johnson's multiple-choice spelling test doesn't "measure up" in terms of validity. In the first place, since it is a multiple choice test, you can't ask the children a question like this:

1. Choose the correct spelling for the word *December.*
   A. December
   B. Dicember
   C. december
   D. January

As you can see, this isn't going to work since the question gives the answer away. If Mr. Johnson tries to fix that situation, he may create other problems of validity:

1. Choose the correct spelling for the twelfth month of the year.
   A. December
   B. december
   C. Desember
   D. January

Unfortunately for Mr. Johnson, the test now measures something other than spelling: Before students identify the correct spelling for the word *December,* they must first identify the twelfth month of the year. Remember that this is a spelling test, not a memory test of whether the child can name the months of the year. Scores on Mr. Johnson's spelling test are invalid because they do not measure what the test is supposed to measure, which is spelling. Both teachers have developed faulty tests that cannot be used effectively.

The reliability and validity of the results of Ms. Peterson and Mr. Johnson's spelling tests become even more questionable when we try to compare the scores of students from each of the teacher's classes. What relationship is there between Ms. Peterson's oral spelling exam and Mr. Johnson's multiple-choice spelling test? Probably none. Since the conditions that both teachers used were very different, comparing the scores is impossible. Look at it this way: Though the children are to spell the twelve months of the year in both classes, a score of 6 in Ms. Peterson's class won't mean the same thing as a score of 6 in Mr. Johnson's class.

To make group comparisons of spelling the months of the year possible, we have to ensure reliability and validity. The tests have to be the same and they have to be given under the same conditions. Here is what Ms. Peterson and Mr. Johnson could do.

1. Develop a spelling test that is reliable. If they have all of the children write the months of the year down on paper from the first to the last month, they are likely to get the same results time after time. Remember that Ms. Peterson's test had problems of reliability since she would get different results from her students each time she said a word and the students spelled it aloud for her individually.
2. Ensure content validity. Mr. Johnson's test did not measure spelling when he asked his students to first name the twelfth month of the year before finding its correct spelling. A test in which the children hear the name of the month and then write it down is a more valid assessment in this case since it tests what it says it tests, spelling the months of the year.
3. Administer reliable and valid assessment tools under the same conditions. As we saw earlier, we could not compare the scores from Mr. Johnson's and Ms. Peterson's classes since the formats and conditions were too different. However, if each teacher sets aside fifteen minutes of class for the test and then reads the test items aloud to the class *once,* before asking the children to write the words down, we would have a score that we could compare. Why? Because the test both teachers used is reliable and valid and because the conditions under which the test was given were the same. This way, a score of 6 in one class means the same thing as a score of 6 in another class, regardless of whether the test was given in Utah or Minnesota.

Now that you have some understanding of what reliability and validity mean, let's take a look at reporting norm-referenced results. The terms that you need to know for norm-referenced reporting include *raw scores, percentile ranks, grade-equivalent scores,* and *scaled scores.* Here is how they might be applied to a spelling test.

1. The raw score on a spelling test is the number correct out of the number of items given. A child who spells six of the twelve months correctly has a score of 6 out of 12.
2. Percentile rankings are different from raw scores. They make comparing the individual to the group, and a group of individuals to other groups of students, much easier. The scale can go from 1–99, and you locate the student's raw score on this scale to figure out how much "better" one student did in relation to other students. A student who spelled all of the items correctly is said to score in the 99th percentile, meaning that she did better than 99 percent of the people who took the test. A student who scored 0 did worse than 99 percent of the people who took the test. Finally, a score in the 50th percentile means that the student did half as well (or half as bad, depending on your perspective) as other students.
3. Grade-equivalent scores move us into the interpretation of what a raw or percentile rank means. For example, if we give our months-of-the-year spelling test over time to second, third, and fourth graders, we can begin to see what "normal" children do in each grade. A raw score of 5 might be normal for second graders and a score of 9 normal for third graders. When you get scores from students in your class, then, you can see whether the child is performing "normally" in relation to other students in the same grade.

All of this should seem quite simple to understand. When you encounter questions about what norm-referenced tests do and do not do, keep this spelling example in mind. Furthermore, if you are asked about how you would report results to parents or other caregivers, keep in mind that they are not experts. Pick answers that are very concrete for parents to understand. For example:

Your child scored in the 99th percentile, yielding an above-average, grade-level equivalent score of 10 out of 12 items. You should be proud.

would need to be amended to

Chris ~~scored~~ got all 12 items right on his spelling test. This means that he scored better than 99 percent of other students who took the test. Since most fourth graders get only 10 items correct on the test, his perfect score means that he is doing better than most children his age. You should be proud.

This way, the information is accessible for parents who probably are not experts in the language of standardized assessments.

Criterion-Referenced Tests.   Criterion-referenced tests are the last type of group assessment that you need to know for the test. The terms associated with these tests include *benchmark* and *rubric* (Ediger, 1999). Like the other assessments described in this section, you have to know how they work, what they tell you about a student's performance, and what is done with the results.

In the first place, criterion-referenced tests look at both product and process. For example, these assessments consider what children are doing when they write the answers that they write, along with whether the answer they've written is correct. Turning to spelling the months of the year again, a criterion-referenced spelling test looks at whether the spellings were correct and at *how* the child spelled the words. The product side of the assessment is handled through the benchmark score for the test, and the process side is viewed through preselected rubric criteria. Here is how it works.

A benchmark score for spelling the months of the year might be set at "12 out of 12" for third graders in the spring of the year. This means that third graders must be able to spell all of the months of the year correctly before they start grade 4. We can up the stakes a bit by stating that children who have not reached this critical benchmark have to repeat third grade until they can do so. Obviously, you would be assessing all of your students from the start of the term to see how far along they were progressing toward that benchmark score so that you could help those students who appeared not to be making progress. This is where the rubric criteria come in.

If a perfect score on spelling the months of the year is the exit criteria for third-grade children, teachers will want to know who is performing at or below these expectations and what to do to help them. Using a rubric can help. Rubrics typically rate students in terms of early, developing, or advanced stages of proficiency. If you assess the children in spelling the months of the year, you can begin to develop a view of which children are early, developing, and advanced based on their score and the *spelling processes* they use. The first item is obvious; the second one needs some explaining.

To achieve a 12 out of 12 on the spelling test, students must not only spell the words correctly but also must capitalize each of the words. The spellings of *January, February,* and *December* have some odd features about them. *January* has an odd vowel pattern (*ua*), *February* has a silent *r*; and *December* ought to have the letter *s* in it, not *c*. Based on this information, spelling development criteria could be set for who is early, developing, and advanced.

EARLY
- Does not capitalize the months of the year or does so infrequently
- Spells the words by dominant sounds only (*dsmbr*)

DEVELOPING
- Capitalizes most of the months of the year correctly
- Shows developing spelling patterns (*desember*)

ADVANCED
- Capitalizes all of the months of the year correctly
- Frequently spells the months of the year correctly, with very few exceptions (*Febuary*)

As you assess the children throughout the year on their way toward spelling all of the months of the year perfectly, you can assess the children with this rubric to see how they are doing and what they need. For example, if you have two children who consistently get a 6 on the spelling test, you can figure out why that is so. For the first child, it might be only because he does not capitalize the months of the year. Fixing that will bring him nearer to the benchmark. For another child, capitalization might not be the issue; instead, it is with spelling -er at the end of some words and with writing all of the sounds not heard in the word (*February*). Criterion-referenced assessments are useful for identifying strengths and needs in children and for helping them to reach particular benchmarks for their development. They take both product and process into account.

A final note is that criterion-referenced assessments can be as minimal as the one described for spelling or as broad as the type that might be used for portfolios. If applied to portfolios, you could use the same type of categories for early, developing, and advanced for a wide variety of areas, including writing style, content, format, grammar, and spelling. As with the spelling example, different indicators would be used to qualify "developing grammar" or "advanced style." Further, the criteria would have to be clear enough so that anyone who rated the portfolios would arrive at roughly the same conclusion.

To this point, the text has described both individual and group assessments of literacy. The next task is to move into the model itself to look at areas of decoding and how they are assessed and instructed. What you learn next is how you will be tested on how children learn to read. You may wish to refer to the model described in Chapter 1 right now to refresh your memory of the overall picture of reading instruction before continuing with these sections.

LEVEL 2: DECODING (KINDERGARTEN THROUGH THIRD GRADE)

This section explains the assessments and activities associated with learning to read. It contains information primarily for kindergarten through third grade, though it also applies to upper-elementary students who have reading difficulties. Read this section with care because it provides the foundation for later instruction in fluency and comprehension.

Overview of Decoding Instruction

The sections that follow cover three areas: the foundations of decoding, explicit phonics instruction, and its ultimate goal of automatic decoding. Let's get an overview of the material first. Table 2.4 shows how all of these areas fit together. As Table 2.4 shows, decoding

TABLE 2.4   Overview of Decoding Instruction

FIRST: FOUNDATIONS OF DECODING		SECOND: EXPLICIT DECODING INSTRUCTION		THIRD: ULTIMATE AIM
Concepts about print	Phonemic awareness	Phonics skills	Sight words	Automatic decoding
DEVELOPMENTAL SPELLING INSTRUCTION (K–8)				

instruction can be divided into three areas (Stahl, 1992), including the foundations of decoding (concepts about print and phonemic awareness), the areas of decoding instruction (phonics skills and sight words), and the ultimate aim of decoding instruction, which is automatic decoding. Spelling instruction spans all areas of this area of the model, from its foundations to its ultimate aim.

The order of the items is fixed. Understanding what comes first, second, and third when answering test questions is important because many of them may ask you what to do first or next when assessing or teaching concepts about print, phonemic awareness, phonics, or spelling. As such, knowing the components of this part of the model well will help you immensely on decoding-related questions. The role that each area plays is presented next. Assessment of and instruction in each of these areas follows this discussion.

Concepts about Print (CAP)

Consider this example: Imagine that there are two children sitting next to one another at a table. Neither child knows how to read yet. You give each child a small pile of books and then observe them from a distance. The child on the left takes the books and creates a small house out of them, while the child on the right begins "pretend reading" by turning the pages, inventing a story based on the pictures in it, and so forth. Which child seems more ready to begin early-reading instruction?

The child on the right is more prepared for early-reading instruction because he did not use the books as ̸ playthings. He has some basic understandings about how books function and what people use them for. The child who built the small house out of the books, on the other hand, needs instruction in some critical areas before the act of reading will make sense.

Concepts about print (CAP) is one part of the foundation for early decoding instruction and is an expectation for kindergarten, though it may progress into first grade. Early CAP assessment and instruction determines if the child knows how to use a book as a tool, not as a toy: for example, if the child can locate the cover, point to the title, and know where to start reading. Later stages of CAP assessment and instruction focus on much smaller elements, such as identifying words and the letters within them. By the end of CAP instruction, it is expected that children are able to recognize all printed upper- and lowercase letters by name, whether in sequence or out of sequence. This skill is very important because once the child can name most upper- and lowercase letters, you can start letter-sound instruction.

How Is CAP Assessed? To understand CAP assessment, you need to know the CAP sequence. Table 2.5 shows what the components look like and their order. Assessments fall

TABLE 2.5 Concepts about Print

Parts of a book	Print carries meaning	Tracking print	Words in sentences	Letters within words	Upper- and lowercase letter names

into the following categories: book concepts, sentence concepts, and word concepts. Following are areas that you should know for the exam.

- Book concepts: Where is the cover? The title? The author's name? The table of contents?
- Sentence concepts: Is the picture or the print read on the page? Where does the reading start from? In which direction is the text read?
- Word concepts: Where do words begin and end? Where is a capital letter?

This pattern makes sense. If your ultimate goals are to have the child use a book as a tool from which to learn and to be able to identify letters and name them, there is a logical sequence of ideas about what has to come first. In the beginning, the child has to learn "book concepts," including the parts of a book (for example, the cover, the title, the author's name, and the table of contents). Furthermore, the child has to learn that when books are read, the sentences are the things that you look at to make the book "work"—it is the print that carries the meaning, not the pictures. Understanding that sentences are made up of words and that words themselves are made up of things called letters are the next major areas of CAP, since these concepts move toward the critical understanding that upper- and lowercase letters have names.

Checklists are the most common forms of assessment for CAP, and they follow the general-to-specific pattern described earlier. The items listed in Table 2.6 reflect the order and the questions or tasks associated with assessing CAP (Gray-Schlegel & King, 1998). On the test, it is important to recognize why this assessment order is necessary so that you can answer questions about how to assess concepts about print or what to do with a child who is struggling with some aspect of it. Assessment is straightforward: It moves from the broadest concepts (for example, identifying the parts of a book) to the more complex (for example, identifying letters and their names).

Letter names can be assessed separately. Usually, the uppercase letters are separated from the lowercase letters. To see if the child actually knows the letters rather than the memorized pattern, each set of letters is often presented out of sequence:

A Q R T B C L N Y
n b i c f o a x p

The student simply reads a line and the teacher scores it on his copy. Letters that the child skips might be circled, and letter confusions are noted above the printed letters. For exam-

TABLE 2.6 CAP Checklist

Parts of a book	Point to the title.
Print carries meaning	Point to where I begin.
Tracking print	Point to each word as I read to you.
Words in sentences	Show me a word.
Letters within words	Show me a capital or lowercase letter.
Letter names	Letter identification test

ple, children may often confuse *p* and *q* and *b* and *d* because they have not learned that the direction of the shapes conveys what letter names they represent to the reader.

Teachers performing CAP assessments with individual children could use the checklist in Table 2.6 and ask the child to perform a series of tasks that move from general to specific. For example, the teacher could hand the child a book spine first and ask her to locate the title (book concepts). The teacher could then show the child a page that has a picture with one line of text and ask, "where should I start reading?" to see if the child points to the sentence or to the picture. The teacher could ask the child to point to each word as it was read it to them (sentence concepts) to see if she understood that individual words are read, that you have to move from one sentence to the next, and so on. Finally, the teacher could have the child locate words and the letters within them. (See Clay 1993a for an exhaustive CAP exam.)

How Is CAP Instructed?   CAP activities follow the same pattern as assessment. You teach book, sentence, and letter concepts to the children. For the exam, you should know several different activities that teach concepts about print since you might be asked about what skills the teacher teaches to her students during certain interactions. The most common activities that teachers use to develop CAP include big book readings, morning messages, language-experience approaches, and letter-name activities. These activities can be used to emphasize different aspects of CAP. The exceptions are activities that teach letter naming, which is often taught in isolation. Letter naming is discussed separately.

- Big book readings: As the name implies, teachers literally use a big book to teach all of the critical aspects of CAP, from book to letter concepts (Park, 1982). Typically, the teacher uses a pointer in the activity, too. Time might be set aside each day for a big book reading in which the teacher begins instruction by having the children find the front of the big book, the title, the author's name, and so forth. First, explicit instruction might be undertaken; later, the children might generate the answers themselves. Within the text, the teacher can point to each word with the pointer. As time moves on, the teacher can also have different students take turns pointing to words as the teacher reads them aloud. Similar activities would take place with identifying words and letters. CAP skills are taught within the context of this small-group activity.

- Morning messages: Teachers conduct CAP instruction through interactive writings with the children (Button, Johnson, & Furgerson, 1996). Morning message activities, for example, begin with the teacher writing a sentence on the board (e.g., *Today is Wednesday*) and either reading the sentence to the students with a pointer or having the students take turns doing so. The teacher and students can also generate a one sentence "story" about what they are going to do that day (e.g., *We are going to the zoo*). At this point, the teacher can instruct which letters need to be capitalized, letter names, word boundaries, and punctuation.

- Language experience approaches (LEAs): LEAs (Taylor, 1992) can be individual activities that ask children to describe experiences that they have had (usually no more than one sentence in the beginning) that the teacher writes down word for word. The teacher and student read the sentence together to teach sentence and word concepts by using the child's language to do so. Later, the child writes the sentence herself, but the same process of reading the sentence together with the teacher takes place. Later, checking the sentence for capital letters and punctuation can take place, along with including appropriate spelling patterns that have been learned in class.

■ Letter-name activities: Letter-name instruction (Woden & Boettcher, 1990) can be done separately. Typically, teachers use a variety of approaches to teach letter names, starting with using an alphabet line, a pointer, and choral recitation of the name of each letter. However, different instructional activities occur for different purposes. Teachers may use pictures of animals or physical actions to accompany letter-name instruction (for example, reciting "A a ape" while mimicking the gestures an ape makes). This helps the children associate specific names or actions to letters, which is helpful when they get stuck on a letter. Also, categorization can be useful during letter-name instruction. Children might sort letters by their characteristics, for instance, grouping magnetic letters according to which ones have holes in them (e.g., *o, d, e*), which have sticks (*l, k, b*), and so on (Clay, 1993b). Such an activity helps the child begin to recognize the letters and attend to their attributes more carefully.

■ Multisensory techniques: Letter confusions are also addressed through specific activities, like multisensory techniques (Vickery, Reynolds, & Cochran, 1987). Multisensory techniques, for example, have children write letters in the air or in sand to help them learn the forms of easily confused letters. Writing activities are also used to help children learn how to form easily confused letters. The letters *b* and *d* can be taught by combining language, writing, and practice. Forming the letter *b* involves moving the pen down, up, and around, while forming the letter *d* can be taught by moving the pen around, up, then down. This helps children learn how to distinguish letters of the alphabet based on how they are written.

As you can see, the end point of CAP instruction is naming upper- and lowercase letters. This ability is essential because the child will eventually attach sounds to those known letters. Learning those individual sounds is the result of instruction in phonemic awareness, the next area discussed.

Phonemic Awareness

Phonemic awareness is the ability to recognize that the English language is made up of individual sounds called phonemes (Yopp & Yopp, 2000). Research indicates that students in the upper grades who are struggling with decoding words lack the ability to break spoken words apart into individual sounds (Hurford & Sanders, 1990). Because the relationship between the ability to break spoken words apart and the ability to read in the later grades is so strong, this model strongly emphasizes phonemic awareness instruction.

There are some terms that need clarification before the discussion proceeds (Chard & Dickson, 1999). First, there is a difference between phonological awareness and phonemic awareness. *Phonology* means "the study of sounds," and *phonological awareness* includes all of the things that one could do to study them, for example, looking at how sounds match or rhyme. *Phonemic awareness,* however, refers to a very specific skill: recognizing that spoken words are made up of individual, identifiable sounds.

Phonemic awareness is vitally important because children learn to have an awareness of the sounds in the English language. Students begin with a general awareness of sounds in the English language. Then they learn to take spoken words and break them into individual sounds, which is called segmenting. Later, they attach letters to these individual sounds and learn how to decode words. Instruction in phonemic awareness occurs for this singular purpose: to prepare children for phonics instruction. This is why the model views segmentation as the highest and most important outcome of instruction in phonological awareness (Ball & Blachman, 1988).

Phonological instruction begins in kindergarten, right alongside CAP. And, like CAP, it begins with very broad concepts and then moves toward a very specific skill: being able to segment spoken words into individual sounds. Children learn about English language sounds through songs, pictures, and activities, including how to perceive and identify sounds heard at word beginnings, how to put sounds together to make spoken words, and how to take spoken words apart in speech. Table 2.7 helps you to see the components of phonemic awareness (Stahl, Duffy-Hester, & Doughtery-Stahl, 1998).

The end points of assessment and instruction lead to one very specific ability: breaking spoken words into individual sounds (Nation & Hulme, 1997). Blending and segmenting are the final areas of phonemic awareness, where children learn to "blend" individual phonemes into spoken words, like /m/-/a/-/n/ = /man/, and to segment spoken words into individual phonemes, like /man/ = /m/-/a/-/n/. (Note: the back slashes indicate sounds, not letters.) Once the child can perform this activity and identify the upper- and lowercase letters of the printed alphabet from CAP instruction, phonics instruction can begin fully by attaching the individual sounds that children can now identify, produce, and manipulate to the letters they learned to identify by name.

One caution is required. Phonemic awareness deals only with spoken words or pictures that represent words (Williams, 1980). The test may try to trick you. Questions about phonemic awareness that introduce any print into the assessments or activities are traps that you must avoid. Any activities that deal with teaching sounds use only sounds; any activities that employ print are considered phonics activities. Keep this distinction absolute. Also, a sound is transcribed as a letter with two back slashes around it. For example, /t/ stands for the sound heard at the beginning of the word *today.* It is not the letter *t.*

Another consideration is the variety of sounds associated with letters. As you now know, phonemic awareness activities deal only with sounds and not letters. Later in this chapter is a full discussion of sound-letter associations, but for now, keep in mind that some letters have different sounds associated with them. For example, the letter *s* has two sounds attached to it: /s/ and /z/, as in *bikes* and *cars.* On the test, you may see data that show how a child might segment a spoken word such as "cars" as /k/ /a/ /r/ /z/. This is correct because the first sound does sound like a /k/ and the final sound does sound like /z/, not /s/.

TABLE 2.7 Phonemic Awareness

Initial and final sound identification	Discriminating sounds in different words	Blending sounds into words	Segmenting spoken words into sounds

How Is Phonological Awareness Assessed?   The most useful pattern for phonemic awareness assessment is as follows.

1. Initial and final sound identification
   - Identifying first and last sounds heard in spoken words
   - Identifying first and last sounds heard in words using picture sorts
2. Discriminating Sounds
   - Differentiating first and last sounds heard in two or more spoken words
   - Differentiating first and last sounds heard in two or more words using picture sorts
3. Blending Sounds
   - Assembling individual sounds into a spoken word
4. Segmenting Spoken Words
   - Disassembling each sound heard in a spoken word

Let's look at each area in greater detail.

Beginning/Ending Sounds.   First, you find out if the child can identify any sounds in the words. Position dominates this assessment since it is easier for most children to identify the first sound heard in a word than it is for them to listen through the word to the final sound. Sounds in the middle part of the word, termed *medial sounds,* tend to be assessed through blending since they are very hard to hear in words and are therefore lost. For example, the sound heard in the middle of the word *car* is the letter name *r.* Medial sounds identification may be assessed by other means. (See Elkonin sound boxes.)

The assessment occurs with spoken words. The teacher says the word *cat* and asks the child what sound is heard at the beginning of each word.

Teacher: What sound do you hear at the beginning of the word *cat?*
Child: /k/
Teacher: What sound do you hear at the end of the word *cat?*
Child: /t/

Pictures can also be used for this assessment. The teacher shows the child a picture and asks him what sound is heard at the beginning or the end. Children who have difficulty articulating sounds can point to other pictures that share the same initial sounds to indicate understanding.

Discriminating Sounds.   The second area of assessment is determining whether the children can tell the difference between the initial or final sounds heard in pairs of words (or triplets). Like identifying beginning sounds in single words, sound discrimination is a very broad skill that helps children to attend to differences in the phonemes that they hear in spoken words. Spoken words are said to the child, who must then decide whether the sounds of the words are the same or different.

Teacher: Tell me if the sounds at the beginning of these words are the same or different: *cat...cow*
Child: Same.

Pictures can be used for this assessment, too. The teacher shows the child pairs of pictures and asks the student to state whether the sounds heard at the beginnings of them are the same or different.

Blending and Segmenting.   The third and fourth levels of phonemic awareness assessment are more challenging for children. Blending and segmenting are more difficult because the child must be able to manipulate individual phonemes, either by assembling them into words by blending the sounds together or segmenting individual sounds from spoken words. When assessing blending, teachers might ask the following.

What word do these sounds make, /k/-/a/-/t/?

Assessing segmenting often occurs as follows.

What sounds do you hear in the word *cat*?

It is important to stress that for each of these assessments, only spoken words or pictures of words are used as prompts. No print is introduced since the idea is to determine if children are ready for phonics instruction based on their ability to segment words into individual sounds.

How Do Teachers Instruct Phonological Awareness?   Picking correct multiple-choice answers or writing correct responses to prompts that are related to phonemic awareness involves knowing the pattern of assessment and the type and structure of activities that correspond to these areas. Keep in mind that the test may not ask you directly about these activities. However, you have to know the general principles of the activities described next so that you can recognize a correct phonemic awareness activity if you are asked to identify one or to describe one in an essay. The order below reflects the activities related to each area of phonemic awareness assessment. Explanations follow for each activity.

1. Initial and final sound identification	Initial/final sorts with picture cards
2. Discriminating sounds in spoken words	Selecting correct pictures from spoken prompts
3. Blending sounds into words	Phoneme blending with picture categories
4. Segmenting words into sounds	Elkonin boxes

Notice that the activities line up with each area of assessment.

■ Identification and matching activities: Sorting pictures of cards by common initial or final sound is an activity that can help to develop a child's ability to identify phonemes. For example, a picture of a cat might be the card at the head of a list. The child would then look at a remaining number of cards and decide whether a picture of a cake, a car, or a bicycle belong beneath the picture of the cat. These activities help the child begin the initial work that is necessary with phonemes in the English language.

■ Sound discrimination activities: Picture cards can also be used to help the child identify and discriminate sounds. Activities for this area can be structured as follows. Using picture cards of words that are phonologically similar, such as *cat, car,* and *can,* the child can sort them into piles by common initial sound or different final sound. Variations on this activity can also be performed. One common variation is to display a series of cards where two of them share common characteristics and one does not (for example, *cat, car, bike*). The child is then asked to identify the picture that does not belong with the other two. Explanations of why responses are correct or incorrect are easier to explain because the pictures can be used as the basis for the explanation.

■ Blending activities: Songs are often used in blending activities, where the teacher sings a series of phonemes and pauses to allow the children to supply the word that the phonemes represent. Readers might be familiar with the song "Bingo" ("B-I-N-G-O"), but singing this song is not a blending activity. "Bingo" is a song that uses letter names, and letter names are not the focus of phonemic awareness activities. Songs that change the first sound of the word in a familiar refrain are used instead.

Picture cards can also be used to teach children how to blend sounds into recognizable spoken words. The teacher can select a category of pictures and teach the children to listen for the correct string of phonemes that match the card. For example, using the category of animals, the teacher could display picture cards of a dog, a cat, a horse, and so on. Then, she could say individual phonemes for the child and ask the child to select the correct card. Both the teacher and child could practice blending and selecting these cards together.

■ Elkonin sound boxes: Elkonin sound boxes (Joseph, 2000a) use markers to help children learn how to segment words into individual phonemes. Typically, a teacher shows the student a picture of a familiar word, says the name of the picture, stretches the sound, and then works with the child to segment the word into individual phonemes (Griffith & Olson, 1992). Segmenting takes place by moving markers into boxes that account for each of the sounds heard in the word. Figure 2.9 shows an example of the spoken word *car*. The teacher would show the picture and say the word for or with the child. Both could practice stretching the sound of the word, before focusing on individual phonemes heard in the word (/k/, /a/, /r/). Markers are then moved up for each sound so that the child can use another sense to learn this skill. Independent practice would follow. Note that for words such

First	Second	Third
●		
↑	●	●

FIGURE 2.9

as *book* or *duck,* only three markers would be used, because the child is marking sounds in the word and not the letters. Letters are not part of phonemic awareness instruction.

To sum up, phonological awareness is taught concurrently with CAP, but this does not mean that they are taught simultaneously. Think of it this way. Teachers do not wait until children have attained a working knowledge of CAP before starting instruction in phonemic awareness. Instead, teachers might take one hour in the morning to teach CAP and the following hour to conduct phonological awareness activities. Both of these areas provide the foundation on which phonics instruction begins. The goal is to assess and instruct the student in the individual sounds of the English language. Once the child can identify and manipulate individual phonemes, as in the segmenting example above, teachers begin instruction in letter-sound correspondence.

Other areas of phonemic awareness assessment may be required. Please visit your state's department of education online and download the standards for kindergarten through second grade. Review the standards carefully and make additions to the table in Appendix B accordingly. Keep in mind that segmenting is always the most important outcome for this model of reading instruction, since it is the essential foundation for later phonics instruction, described next.

Early, Late, and Advanced Phonics Instruction

Phonics instruction begins fully when the child performs the highest levels of concepts about print and phonemic awareness with ease (Chall, 1996). You can look at the starting point of phonics instruction as a convergence of the end points of CAP and phonemic awareness instruction. Since the child can name most upper- and lowercase letters from CAP and can also manipulate individual sounds, then letter-sound correspondence can begin.

Table 2.8 reflects the most important areas of phonics instruction. The order of items in the table is important, and you should memorize it. The table begins with letter-sound correspondence. While the child has learned letter names in CAP and sound segments in spoken words from phonemic awareness, he may not yet know how to put the two areas together. For example, without letter-sound instruction, it is possible that a child would decode the written word, *car* as *seeayar,* and it will make the process of learning to decode slow and cumbersome.

The remaining areas of the model, onset-rime instruction, phonics generalizations, and polysyllabic word decoding, represent early to advanced areas of decoding, instruction that the discussion turns to next (high-frequency sight words are addressed separately). Keep in mind that the ultimate goal of decoding instruction is the fluent and automatic decoding of print. Once fluent decoding is in place, instruction can focus on comprehension and reading to learn fully.

TABLE 2.8   Phonics and Decoding Instruction

Letter-sound correspondence	Onset-rime instruction	Phonics generalizations	Polysyllabic word decoding	High-frequency sight words

In the next sections, you will see that early phonics instruction begins with the *alphabetic principle,* where one letter represents one sound and the child learns to decode simple, one-syllable words. Later phonics instruction moves beyond this narrow definition so that the child learns to decode more complicated words with still-common letter combinations. Advanced phonics instruction has the child decoding words by phonics generalization (that is, by rule) and by complex consonant and vowel combinations on the way toward working with polysyllabic word decoding.

Early Phonics Instruction.   Early phonics instruction teaches the child to associate sounds to letters and to combine these letters into short, common, one-syllable words that are easily decoded. Once the child has a few known sound-letter associations, these letters become "onsets" that are attached to other simple letter patterns called rimes to make words. Onsets and rimes are easiest to recognize in any one-syllable, consonant-vowel-consonant word. For example, *cat, hat, mat, sat,* and *rat* all share the same rime (*-at*), but different onsets (*c, h, m, s,* and *r*). The onset is the first consonant or the consonant in the "front part" of a one-syllable word, and the rime is the "back part" (the vowel and maybe a consonant—*ma* is a one-syllable word with *m* as its onset and *a* as its rime).

How Are Early Phonics Skills Assessed?   Early phonics assessment and instruction centers around letter-sound associations and simple onset-rime decoding. Let's start with letter-sound assessment. Early letter-sound assessments can be performed with and without print. Assessments that use no print can be carried out as follows:

> **Teacher:**   Tell me the sound you hear at the start of this word and the first letter: *cat.*
> **Student:**   /s/ ... *c.*

This is very abstract, however, and there are more concrete assessments available. Assessments that use print can be conducted in the same manner that the alphabet recognition test from CAP was performed, only the teacher asks the student to supply sounds for each of the words, either instead of or in addition to the letter names. As you can imagine, breaking the child of reciting the letter name usually presents a challenge.

Assessing a child's ability to decode short, one-syllable words occurs with lists of words with common onsets and rimes. For example, words from the *-at* or *-an* family (*cat, sat, rat* and *tan, man, fan*) can be used to assess the student's ability to decode both the common onset and rime. Short sentences can also be used for this purpose, provided that the child has been taught to decode both the letter patterns in the sentence and the sight words in the sentences (see High-Frequency Sight Words later in this section).

Later Phonics Instruction.   Sound-letter associations become more complex as phonics instruction advances since often combinations of letters are used to represent a wide range of sounds (for example, *th-, -igh, -ough*). Consider the following.

bl-	blend, bliss, block
th-	thank, think, thumb
-ack	rack, sack, tack

As children learn more and more sound associations, they can begin to handle more and more complex onset and rime letter combinations. Using consonant blend and digraph combinations are common during later phonics instruction. To remember your blends and digraphs, memorize the following.

- The *bl* in *blend* is a blend because you can hear both sounds associated with both letters.
- The *ph* in *digraph* is a digraph because the *p* and the *h* come together to make an entirely different sound (we don't say *digra-pa-huh*).

Instruction in decoding words that use these combinations begins in isolation, before appearing in decodable text. Because the same types of assessments and activities used to teach simple onsets and rimes apply to these complex onset and rime combinations, the text does not describe any specific tests or activities for these later phonics elements.

Advanced Phonics Instruction. Advanced phonics instruction focuses on generalizations (that is, rules) and complex vowel patterns. Before looking at the common assessments and activities associated with these areas, generalizations and vowel patterns are explained first.

Common Phonics Generalizations. The most common phonics generalizations are as follows.

- CVC short vowel patterns
- CVCe long vowel patterns
- Hard and soft *g*
- Hard and soft *c*

Consonant-vowel-consonant (CVC) and consonant-vowel-consonant-silent *e* (CVCe) patterns affect the length of the vowel sound found between the consonants. Usually, the CVC pattern makes the vowel short, like *hat, met, pin, not.* If a silent *e* is added to these CVC words, the vowel becomes long or "says its name": *hate, mete, pine, note.* Whether the letters *g* and *c* are hard, as in *game* and *cat,* or soft, as in *gym* or *city,* depends on the vowels that follow these letters. For example, the letters *a* and *o* make the *c* words hard, like *cat, cake,* and *cot.* The letters *i* and *y,* on the other hand, make *c* words soft, like *city* and *cytoplasm.* The word *garage* is another good example since it contains both the hard and soft *g* in it.

Complex Vowel Representations.
- Long vowel digraphs
- Vowel blends (diphthongs)

Vowel representations are very complex in English, and we have a number of ways to mark long and "diphthongized" vowel sounds in words. Long vowels can be represented in a number of different ways.

a: ray, rain, feign
e: each, beat, feet
i: lie, buy, thigh

The above long vowel representations are vowel digraphs. Just like with consonant digraphs, two vowels or a vowel and other letters come together to represent one sound. Vowel blends also exist, though we call them diphthongs. Diphthongs are "like consonant blends [and] consist of two vowels in one syllable where two sounds are heard" (Cooper & Kiger, 2003, p. 508). Cooper and Kiger (2003) identify the diphthongs that occur most frequently as *oi, oy, ou,* and *ow.* They also draw an important distinction between vowel digraphs and vowel diphthongs:

Vowel digraph	beet, meat, piece, weigh
Vowel diphthong	boil, joy, out, cow

Unlike vowel digraphs, vowel diphthongs represent two individual and distinguishable vowel sounds.

How Are Later and Advanced Phonics Skills Assessed?   The same assessments that characterized assessment of early phonics skills apply here too. Students read words from lists in each area and the teacher marks the areas of need for each type of word. The starting point for instruction begins at the decoding level at which the child is struggling. For example, it is possible that the child is proficient when decoding simple onset-rime combinations but has difficulty with specific phonics generalizations. Instruction would then center on the generalizations. Furthermore, instruction would also try to make a connection between generalizations to the next level of phonics instruction, which is to decode words with more complex letter combinations.

How Are Early, Late, and Advanced Phonics Skills Instructed?   Early, late, and advanced phonics skills are instructed explicitly and directly through activities that require children to attend to print. Explicit instruction means that particular features of words are emphasized through color or other means. The words are also isolated and taken out of their context for instruction. Direct instruction describes the role of both the teacher and the student during instruction.

Here, the teacher preteaches the feature or the rule that the student is to learn. Then, the teacher and student practice identifying the feature or applying the rule together. Finally, the student practices the skill alone while the teacher observes and evaluates the student's progress. The application phase usually takes places within the context of a sentence that uses words, features, or rules that have been practiced previously in decodable text. The explicit and direct activities in which children engage place little to no emphasis on context in this model since the goal is to teach children to rely on text to identify words. Here, comprehension is viewed as a separate area of instruction.

The most useful phonics activity for the exam is called the word sort (Morris, 1982). It can be used to instruct children to decode words by simple onset and rime, phonics generalization, or complex consonant or vowel pattern. Word sorts are the easiest activities to recognize and use for the test because they ask children to focus on letters and patterns to make or categorize words during explicit phonics instruction. Keep in mind that you are not simply learning about word sorts here. Instead, you are trying to learn about principles that you can extend to any questions that deal with instructing children in phonics. The lesson plan for this type of instruction is described in Chapter 3. Though it describes a word sort used to develop spelling, it can be easily adapted to most of the activities described next.

■ **Letter-sound instruction:** Letter-sound instruction can begin with picture books, where the teacher preselects pictures of familiar animals, objects, and even actions to associate with each of the letters of the alphabet. For example, the letter *a* can represent a picture of an ape, which makes sense since the word shares the same initial sound as the letter. However, a picture of a short vowel word can also be used (for example, *apple*) to teach the child to associate both long and short vowel sounds with this letter. The visual or other sensory associations are important in this model. They allow teachers to use these associations to prompt students when they encounter letters in isolation or in words in which they cannot remember the sounds.

Teacher: (points to the letter *j*):   What letter is this?

Student: I don't know.

Teacher (prompts):   Jay likes to…

Student: Jump! *J!*

■ **Picture/word sorts:** Sorting pictures and words by initial and final consonants sounds is another way to link letter-sound correspondences. Very early instruction would have children sort pictures cards under different letters of the alphabet to help them to develop some sense of letter-sound correspondence. Later, children would sort actual words into different categories to ensure that they are able to sort words based on the initial letters that they see. For example, sorting the words *car, cake,* and *cat* by initial letter is relatively easy; however, sorting the words *city* and *cereal* would add an additional challenge since it might be tempting to sort these words under *s*.

■ **Word walls:** Word walls can also be effective for this purpose (Wagstaff, 1997/1998). Pictures of words with initial sounds can be tacked up under capital and lowercase letters on the word wall. Similarly, as children encounter words in print during big book readings and elsewhere, the words can be tacked under letters on a chart at the front of the classroom. These words can be incorporated into writings or as part of a daily word-wall reading. Word walls are described in greater detail later in this chapter.

■ **Simple onset-rime decoding:** Sorting words by adding onsets and rimes is another very common early activity to instruct decoding explicitly. Common rimes, including *-at* and *-an,* naturally take onsets that can be used for instruction (for example, *cat, hat, mat*). The goal of instruction is to help children to pay careful attention to words that use these common rimes and to be able to decode them when they are found in print.

■ **Word building with phonics rules:** As discussed earlier, phonics generalizations are rules for spelling certain words. For example, changing the word *cap* into the word *cape* requires the addition of silent *e* to the end of the word, making the medial vowel become long or "say its name." Sorting words by rule is another viable option to help children to acquire knowledge of highly applicable phonics rules. The general description of the word sort applies here, too. Hard and soft *c* and *g* can be taught the same way.

■ **Spelling activities:** Spelling activities are used to support instruction in the early, later, and advanced areas of phonics and decoding. Teachers use specific types of spelling activities to transition students from early to late to advanced phonics. These activities are examined in greater detail later in this section.

Polysyllabic Word Decoding

Decoding words with open and closed syllables is critical because the type of vocabulary that the children encounter in the upper-elementary grades is polysyllabic. Further, the words are harder in terms of what they mean and how they convey that meaning structurally. Take *antidisestablishmentarianism* as an example. If children are going to be able to read words like these, and understand them, then they will need to learn how to decode words with open and closed syllables in the early grades.

Recognizing open and closed syllables is easy. Put your hand under your chin and say the word *mama*. Every time your chin went down, it marked a syllable. Now, look at the syllables in the word: *ma* and *ma*. You should notice that your jaw dropped on each voiced vowel. Since no consonant follows the vowel in each rime, we say that it is open. Contrast this with the word *Batman*. There are two syllables (*bat* and *man*), but this time they are closed since there is a consonant in the rime. Look back to the opening example, *antidisestablishmentarianism,* and you can see that the child needs to know how to pick it apart for its open and closed syllables to decode it correctly.

Following are four different types of polysyllabic words that you should know for the test (Olsen & Ames, 1972, as quoted in Vacca & Vacca, 1989, p. 327):

1. Compound words, such as *batman, toolbox,* and *weathermen*
2. Complex words with prefixes and suffixes, such as *unrecognizable* and *antidisestablishmentarianism*
3. Decodable words, such as *calculus* and *elephant*
4. Irregular words, such as *Wednesday* and *February*

Training students to decode polysyllabic words is also important for another reason, beyond the fact that these words are more demanding. In upper-elementary grades, children read expository text. Expository text is informational text that can be found in social studies or science. The vocabulary found in informational text is more demanding because it tends to be polysyllabic and may also require other skills to be comprehensible. *Antidisestablishmentarianism* requires a series of skills if an upper-elementary student is to both *decode* and *understand* it. The first step in being able to understand words such as these in the upper-elementary grades is to have the skill of decoding polysyllabic words in place by the end of third grade.

How Are Polysyllabic Words Assessed?   Syllabication is the final area of phonics instruction that sets the stage for fluently decoding text that grows more and more complex in the upper-elementary grades. Obviously, word lists with polysyllabic words are used in much the same way that sight word assessments are carried out. However, another important type of word is often used that you should know about for the test. Pseudo- or non-sense words are typical assessment words that determine whether the child can decode polysyllabic words effectively. Table 2.9 shows examples of nonsense words that use open and closed syllables. The goal of such pseudo-word assessments is to ensure that the child can decode words with both open and closed syllables, without being "distracted" by trying to comprehend the words that are "reading." Any deficiencies in decoding these words are noted and instruction is then prescribed according to the area of need (open syllables only, closed syllables only, and so on).

How Are Polysyllabic Words Instructed?   Instruction in decoding polysyllabic words involves aspects of phonemic awareness and print. The reason that this instruction tends to be conducted later in phonics instruction is that children must be proficient in recognizing letters and basic letter patterns if decoding polysyllabic words is going to make sense to them.

Teaching students to analyze and decode words based on syllable structure involves removing polysyllabic words from the text and conducting explicit instruction in how to decode them. Following are guidelines (adapted from Cunningham, 1978; Cunningham, 1980; Vacca & Vacca, 1989):

TEACHER PREPARATION
1. Preselect a list of polysyllabic words that can be decoded successfully.
2. Write the words on note cards and emphasize each of divisions within the word by underlining, dividing, or highlighting them.
3. Develop sentences that use known words around the targeted polysyllabic words. Do not highlight the polysyllabic word or provide any other prompts since these sentences will be used for assessment.
4. Using the note cards, teach the students that polysyllabic words can be divided into decodable units.

TEACHER MODELING
5. Model methods of decoding the words on the note cards. Use a pointer under each syllable of the word as it is pronounced, clap each syllable out for the student, or place the hand under the chin as the word is read (each chin drop marks a syllable in the word).
6. Model how to reassemble the word into one spoken utterance. Slide the pointer beneath the word smoothly as it is pronounced.

TABLE 2.9   Pseudo-words

OPEN-OPEN	CLOSED-CLOSED	OPEN-CLOSED	CLOSED-OPEN
taza	nemtis	ranib	piptee
rala	tolgap	mogup	quampo
jabi	vabmot	fazil	blastoe

GUIDED PRACTICE
7. Practice the strategy with the student to ensure proficiency.

INDEPENDENT PRACTICE
8. Use the prewritten sentences to test whether the student effectively uses this skill for polysyllabic words.

Polysyllabic word decoding is the last and highest level of phonics instruction in this model. It combines all of the previous areas of decoding, from letter-sound correspondence to complex letter patterns. It is also the segue into reading comprehension through higher-level vocabulary instruction.

It is important for you to consult your state's standards to see what the stated sequence is for each of these areas. The patterns increase in complexity by grade, though each state may show some variation in the type of words and the expectations for each grade level. Please consult your state's standards for phonics instruction and compare it with the information presented in this chapter and use it to complete the table in Appendix B.

High-Frequency Sight Word Instruction

High-frequency sight words are words that children must be able to identify in seconds. Many cannot be decoded using the phonics generalizations. These words represent several common high-frequency sight words:

the
where
which
here
who
when
in
on
of

Instruction in sight words occurs very early. As with CAP and phonological awareness, sight word instruction can often be taught separately from phonics instruction in special activities. Since children must read these sight words quickly, please note that sight word instruction is just as important as learning to decode is. For example, once children transition to decodable print to practice a specific phonics skill, they are not going to get very far unless they can read sight words easily and automatically. Consider the sentence below.

The cat sat **on the** mat **by a** rat **that** had **a** hat.

The sight words are in bold. Given their frequency, children have to know them well to read sentences efficiently. But because they are not easily decodable like regularly patterned words are, sight word instruction is handled by a distinct set of assessments and activities. One important note is that sight word instruction constitutes the foundation of many reading programs in which children are taught to recognize a certain number of words before they are taught to read sentences. This model does not favor this type of instruction. Instead, the goal is to teach students to rely on letters from the start, while teaching high-frequency words through automatic recognition. Thus, while both decoding skills and sight vocabularies are taught, this model favors explicit instruction in phonics skills from the very beginning.

How Are High-Frequency Sight Words Assessed?   Sight word assessment is typically carried out in using lists of words. Children read the words from a column that corresponds to grade-level expectations. For example, reading *in* and *the* might occur earlier than reading *where* and *there*. Assessment also occurs when running record and informal reading inventory data are analyzed. For the test, pay careful attention to data sets that have informal reading inventory data since sight word problems may be reflected in the student errors.

How Are Sight Words Instructed?   Sight word instruction can take place in both informal and formal settings. One informal way to teach sight words is during big book readings or morning messages: When the students encounter them, the teacher adds them to the word wall and then uses them during sorting or writing activities (Wagstaff, 1997/1998). However, you need to be able to recognize the characteristics of effective sight word activities. They are roughly the same as the ones described for word sorts (Hennings, 2002).

TEACHER MODELING
1. Isolate the sight words to be taught to the student through specific assessments or through observational records.
2. Write the words for the student on individual index cards and present them to the student in a pocket chart.
3. Model how to read the sight word for the child, beginning with the initial consonant, vowel, or cluster and read through the word. Point out any difficult parts of the word to the child.

GUIDED PRACTICE
4. Work together with the child to learn how to recognize these words by letter combination, pattern (for example, how *here* becomes *where*), and direction (for example, for easily confused words such as *how* and *who*).
5. Teach strategies such as using the index finger to focus attention on the initial letter pattern and reading "through" the word by running the finger beneath it as it is read.
6. Use multisensory techniques, such as tracing letter patterns in sand, to reinforce the visual letter cues.

INDEPENDENT PRACTICE
7. Have the student apply these techniques on preselected text that use these isolated sight words.
8. Use flashcards for the problematic sight words and sort them by common feature.

The idea behind these activities is to involve isolation, attention, context, application, and as many senses as possible in the instruction of sight words (McNinch, 1981), since they may not follow regular decoding patterns and may not stick in the student's memory.

Spelling Development

One area of instruction that spans kindergarten and beyond is spelling instruction. This section describes spelling instruction for primary and upper-elementary students that you need to know for the test. The terminology associated with spelling instruction is presented first before examples of analysis and instructional methods are described.

The terms *pre-phonetic, phonetic, transitional,* and *conventional* are used in many of the test registration bulletins to characterize the spelling stage in which a student's spelling can be categorized. An important idea is that children move through each of these stages on their way to becoming proficient in this area of the model. The following are characteristics for each stage that you should know for the test (adapted from Bear & Barone, 1989; Bear & Templeton, 1998; Invernizzi, Abouzeid, & Bloodgood, 1997).

- The *pre-phonetic stage* describes the spelling that one sees in the writing of children who have little to no knowledge of spelling. Here, children often scribble when asked to spell words because they have not yet learned to associate the sounds that they hear with letters. Later, the scribbling may include discernable lines or symbols that look like regular print. This reflects a child's emerging awareness of the symbolic nature of language.
- The *phonetic stage* starts when children begin to write letters to represent the dominant sounds they hear in words. This stage depends greatly on how much prior knowledge and instruction they have had in encoding orthographic letter patterns. Sounds pretty serious, huh? All that it means is that children can form the appropriate letters based on the sounds they hear and write common letter combinations down.
- The *transitional stage* represents a level in which children encode all of the dominant sounds they hear in the word and attempt to include the complexities found in words. Spelling a word such as *bread* as *brade* is an example of this stage of development, since the child is attempting to encode a complicated vowel digraph (*ea*) by adding a silent *e* to the end of the word. This stage reflects very late development and is a goal of instruction.
- The *conventional stage* in spelling is the stage in which children spell correctly the majority of words they write. This does not mean that they spell every word correctly, though. Common misspellings at this stage include words such as *independ*ance and *confid*ant. In the upper-elementary grades, children at this stage of development use spelling to increase vocabulary, particularly content-area vocabularies, as they learn to spell words that use prefixes, suffixes, and roots. A full discussion of this area of spelling instruction takes place when vocabulary instruction is covered later in this chapter.

Be sure to check your registration bulletin carefully since the terms may vary a bit. The concepts are exactly the same, however, so you will have no trouble in using either the terms from the bulletin or the terms in this text.

Table 2.10 illustrates spellings that typify each stage of development (all data are hypothetical).

Each of the spelling data for the words, *tree, cars,* and *bread,* reflect the spelling stages that you need to know for the test. The first example (pre-phonetic) for *tree* shows

TABLE 2.10 Spelling Development Stages

PRE-PHONETIC	PHONETIC	TRANSITIONAL	CONVENTIONAL
⟡	tr	Tre	*tree*
⌇⌇⌇	Krz	carz	*cars*
⟁⟂	Brd	brade	*bread*

that the child moves from scribbling to encoding (writing) the most dominant sounds heard in the word, which is the consonant blend *tr.* In the transitional stage, the child successfully encodes all of the dominant sounds heard in the word. The student needs instruction in encoding long vowel patterns to move into the conventional stage.

The second example (phonetic) for *cars* shows that the child moves from scribbling to encoding all of the major sounds heard in the word. However, the letter *k* that is used to mark the hard *c* sound and the *r*-controlled vowel is missing. These factors keep the spelling at the phonetic level. In the last stage, the child has encoded all of the sounds heard in the word but still is confused about how to encode the final consonant *s*. The letter *s* is often heard as a /z/ or an /ez/, depending on the letters that precede it. Instruction in encoding the final *s* correctly is necessary to move the child into the conventional stage.

The last example (transitional), *bread,* shows the child moving from scribbling to encoding the major sounds heard in the word. The transitional spelling, *brade,* is very interesting. The child knows that there is something strange about the way the medial vowel sound is spelled and tries to capture it by adding a silent *e* to the end of the word. Instruction in patterns is necessary to move the child into the conventional stage.

Note that all of the pre-phonetic spellings for each of the words (*tree, cars,* and *bread*) show different levels of progress, even in the scribbling. The pattern moves from the pre-phonetic spelling for *tree* to the pre-phonetic spelling for *bread.* The first scribbling shows little progress in attempting to write, since there are no recognizable shapes that look like print. The second scribbling for *cars* actually shows some progress, because there is a discernable pattern to the waves in the lines. The third pre-phonetic spelling, however, shows the most progress. There are some identifiable symbols that the child is using to represent unknown letters. This shows that the writer has some understanding of the symbolic nature of language.

Spelling instruction in this model is best understood as follows. Effective instruction means that the teacher moves the child from one stage to another through different sets of activities. For example, transitioning a child from the pre-phonetic spelling stage to the phonetic spelling stage requires very specific types of activities. In the first place, the child has to learn to encode simple letters by name or sound before they are able to attach those letters to sounds heard in words that they are asked to spell. The same idea is true for moving students from phonetic spelling to transitional spelling. For example, children have been taught to move from encoding dominant sounds heard in words (phonetic stage) to encoding complex medial-vowel patterns to move into the transitional spelling of the *ea* in *bread.* In short, it is important for you to recognize each of these stages are goals of instruction and that activities are meant to bridge the gap between them.

How Is Spelling Assessed?   Most spelling programs use lists of words that follow the patterns of the phonics model described earlier. The words increase in complexity as the letter combinations and generalizations become more and more complex. The data can be interpreted in a variety of ways, including raw scores and criterion reference. Let's look at how spelling is assessed through a transitional model.

Pre-phonetic	From scribbling to encoding specific sounds
Phonetic	From encoding initial and final sounds to medial sounds
	Encoding sight words
Transitional	From encoding all dominant sounds to writing letter patterns
Conventional	From patterns to derivational affix and complex word family writing

The expectations for each area guide the assessments carried out with children. Pre-phonetic spellers tend to populate kindergarten classrooms, so teaching them to encode letters by name and by sound are common. By the beginning and middle of first grade, children might be assessed on their ability to encode beginning and final sounds, as well as common sight words and short one-syllable words such as *cat* and *dog.* By the end of first grade and into the remaining primary grades, the emphasis is on assessing the child's ability to encode all sounds, as well as sounds that are not heard in words (complex medial vowel patterns, silent *e* words, and so on). Upper-elementary children might be assessed on their ability to spell words with complex letter patterns correctly, along with common suffixes such as *-ation, -ion,* and *-ment.*

Spelling activities in this model are designed to move children from one stage of development to another. The following activities illustrate these transitional goals.

How Is Spelling Instructed?   Recall that the goal of spelling instruction is to move the child from one stage to another. Following are activities that illustrate how this process works in this model (Bear & Barone, 1989; Bear & Templeton, 1998; Invernizzi, Abouzeid, & Gill, 1996/1997).

Pre-Phonetic to Phonetic Spelling.

1. *Writing by "chunk":* Chunks are memorized and probably unanalyzed words that the child can write independently. During the pre-phonetic stage, teaching children to write their names is a common starting point. Children may be able to write their names but not use any of the letters to encode other words that contain the same sounds and letters. The children's names can be used as a point of departure to teach the letters and sounds that they can encode unconsciously. These letters can then be attached to other words that use the same letters in spelling.

2. *Sequenced instruction:* Children may also be taught letter formations through sequences to continue the transition out of pre-phonetic spelling. For example, the letters *o, c, a,* and *e* share similar formation patterns. Teachers may use this sequence when teaching children to write them. However, letters that are easily confused such as *p, b, q,* and *d* are not taught together. Instead, they might be paired with other known letters that differ greatly from the confused letters and then taught separately (for example, *p* and *w, b* and *v, q* and *n, d* and *y*).

Phonetic to Transitional Spelling. Recall that sound boxes are used to teach segmenting during phonemic awareness. The same process can be used to teach children to move from the phonetic to transitional stage through word boxes. Here, the markers used for the activity are changed to letter tiles that the child selects and uses for the activity (Joseph, 2000b). Figure 2.10 shows an example.

First, the teacher and student segment the word (based on the picture) into its individual sounds. Then, the child moves letter tiles into the spaces above to mark each space. The teacher might accept incorrect letters (for example, the letter for a hard *c*) in the beginning, but accuracy is the focus later on. The last part of this activity is to have the child write the words that he has created with the tiles to make it a true spelling activity. The sequence follows the same pattern described for early decoding instruction.

Transitional to Conventional Spelling. Word families are common for this stage of spelling development (Schlagal & Schlagal, 1992). Children learn to write lists of words under different headings to learn to spell by pattern (Invernizzi, Abouzeid, & Bloodgood, 1997).

ee	meet, greet, beet
ea	each, reach, teach
ie	piece, niece, thief
silent *e*	came, tame, same
wh-	where, who, what

The same type of activity can be used to teach doubling and dropping consonants.

-ing	hopping, running, hitting
drop *e, y*	smiling, dried, cried

First	Second	Third
C		

FIGURE 2.10 Word Boxes

As you can see, the model uses spelling patterns as a means to support and reinforce what the children are learning as part of decoding instruction. However, spelling is *not* the primary means of teaching decoding. In this model, children learn to decode primarily through decoding instruction. Spelling is, of course, an important reinforcement and grows more and more important as the child progress from basic decoding to fluency.

Spelling within the Conventional Stage.   Later stages of spelling teach children to spell using Greek and Latin roots and prefixes and suffixes (DiStephano & Hagerty, 1985). Word families again are a viable method for the test.

ann-	annual, anniversary, annum
tele-	telephone, television, telex
im-	impossible, improbable, impermissible
-ation	derivation, renovation, syncopation

Roots and affixes are covered later in this chapter's discussion of vocabulary instruction as part of reading comprehension. Please also refer to your state's standards for spelling instruction (K–8) and complete the table in Appendix B.

With the foundations of decoding covered, the next level of the model is fluent decoding, the ultimate goal of decoding instruction. It has its own activities that you should know for the test.

LEVEL 3: FLUENCY

Fluency is the ultimate aim of decoding instruction (Adams, 1990). The expectation in this model is that children are able to read text "fluently and accurately" by grade 3 (Stahl & Kuhn, 2002). This ability is contingent on the child's ability to recognize words automatically, whether the words follow regular word patterns or not (Adams & Bruck, 1995). One expectation on the test is that you understand that fluency itself must be instructed. Just because a child can read each and every word in a text does not guarantee that he will do so with the fluency that is required at this level of the model, so you have to be well versed in the correct activities to develop this very important skill.

The reason that fluency is so important in this model has to do with comprehension (Rasinski, 2000). Throughout this chapter, it is stated that decoding skills are important because children who spend their time making and correcting errors are not able to comprehend what they are reading. Time and attention are two critical factors here: Making and correcting errors takes time and attention away from understanding, which explains all of the emphasis on decoding in the early grades. So, instruction in fluency really is the gateway that marks the distinction between the end of learning to read and the beginning of reading to learn.

Keep in mind that some children acquire fluency much earlier than other students. For such children, their attention can then focus on vocabulary and comprehension, rather than on decoding and fluency only. Be sure to look at data sets this way on the test. Though the grade level might only be first, the child might be fluent and, therefore, able to focus on vocabulary and comprehension. In short, refer to both the grade level and the fluency level for reference.

How Is Fluency Assessed?

Fluency is assessed in terms of rate and accuracy. The easiest way to calculate a fluency rate is to have a child read a long passage of grade-level text, or text that should be at the independent reading level, for one minute. You then count the words that the child read during that period. There is a great variance around the country for how many words are to be read at a particular grade level, so refer to your state's standards for the appropriate levels. If your state does not offer any specifics, it might not be part of the exam.

The second area, accuracy, is important. A person who can type one hundred words per minute might impress you; however, if the same person types an equal number of mistakes in each word, you might not be impressed at all. The same is true for reading accuracy and fluency: You have to have some idea of how accurately the child reads the passage, not just how quickly. The informal reading inventories and the running records described in assessment (see Level 1) are fine ways to calculate accuracy. The same percentages for independent, instructional, and frustration levels apply to accuracy rates here. See the section entitled Reading Passages for the example assessment.

How Is Fluency Developed?

In this model, fluency is developed through practice. The belief is that this skill can be instructed, so it is important for you to know the most common activities that are used in its development. You can divide fluency activities into two different groups. There are teacher-directed activities and there are other activities that the student undertakes independently. Table 2.11 captures each of these types of activities and their characteristics.

The following are explanations of each type of activity that you should know for the test.

Choral Reading Activities to Build Expression.   Choral reading (McCauley & McCauley, 1992) is a teacher-led activity carried out with a small group of students who need help with intonation and "making reading sound like speaking." Ideally, all of the students in the choral reading group share basically the same need so that they acquire the skill that the teacher is modeling for them. Choral reading can take place with a big book that is propped on an easel in front of the children or with individual copies of some text the teacher is reading distributed to every member of the small group.

TABLE 2.11   Fluency

TEACHER-DIRECTED READING		INDEPENDENT/AT-HOME READING	
Choral reading	Repeated reading	Sustained silent reading (SSR)	At-home reading

Modeling is the primary means of instruction. The teacher reads a sentence aloud from the big book or her copy of the text and the students repeat it (echo reading) or the group reads the passage together as a "chorus." The following are general guidelines that you can use to write answers to essay questions or to identify correct multiple-choice items regarding fluency-building activities (Barrentine, 1996).

TEACHER PREPARATION

1. Preselect students who share the same or very similar needs for the choral reading activity.
2. Select a passage that is accessible to all of the children in the group (for example, that is not at a frustration reading level for them).
3. Mark the passage to highlight intonation patterns or other areas of emphasis (for example, punctuation) so that the children have visual cues to help prompt them in their expressive reading.

TEACHER MODELING

4. Give each child a copy of the text.
5. Carry out the reading and model the behavior that you want the children to acquire. For example, if the goal is to teach children to pause at commas, stop at periods, and raise the voice for question marks, your expressive reading must model this for the children.

GUIDED PRACTICE

6. Choral-read the passage together with the students.

INDEPENDENT PRACTICE

7. Listen as the students read back to you with expression and note how individual children perform the activity.

These activities also have the important effect of reducing anxiety. Since children who are having difficulty reading with expression may feel embarrassed practicing in front of more capable peers, choral reading may be an important key to success since the child will feel part of the group and not alone on stage.

Repeated Reading.   Repeated reading (Samuels, 1997) is another teacher-led activity that is designed for individual students. The teacher must know not only the student's independent reading level, but also which books the student has read several times and enjoyed. Ideally, each child has a small collection of high-interest, independent-level books that can be used for this purpose. The goal of this activity is to help students become more and more fluent by reading and rereading text that they are guaranteed to be successful with.

The general steps for the activity are as follows (Gunning, 2003; Tompkins, 2003; Vacca et al., 2003):

1. Determine the student's independent reading level. This procedure is described at the beginning of this chapter.
2. Maintain a collection of books that you know the student can read successfully. Time might be set aside each day to work with individual students on independent-level books to develop such a collection.

3. Test the student's current rate of speed and accuracy at the beginning of the week on a passage from one of the books.
4. Have the student read from the book aloud to you or silently to herself each day from her collection of the texts.
5. Test the student's current rate of speed and accuracy at the end of the week using the same passage that was tested at the start of the week.

Repeated readings build confidence in the same way that choral reading does. It ensures success and reduces frustration. The next activity is an individual one for building fluency.

Sustained Silent Reading. Sustained silent reading (SSR) (Krashen, 1993; Trelease, 1995) is a student-directed reading activity in which children self-select their own materials for reading during a defined period of time. The idea is that children become strong, fluent readers by reading; as such, getting them motivated to read is an important endeavor. SSR capitalizes on student interest since the children pick the books that they want to read during this activity. This activity might help motivate students who read well but are reluctant to do so because they choose high-interest materials. Struggling readers, too, select books from either their familiar collection or new books that are at their independent reading level.

For SSR, the teacher may set aside one-half hour per day during which everyone in the class stops what he or she is doing and reads a self-selected book for a set time period. Following are common guidelines that you should know about SSR.

1. Student reading interest surveys should be conducted early in the year to help the teacher to find materials that this particular group of students wants to read. Materials can also be brought from the child's home, if possible.
2. A wide variety of genres (narrative, short stories, and informational texts) must be available for the children. Further, books, anthologies, magazines, and so on should be available to the children. This ensures that each child finds high-interest reading materials.
3. Materials that represent each child's independent reading level must be included in the collections so that each child succeeds in this activity.
4. The same time should be designated each day for SSR so that the children have their materials chosen prior to the start of the session.
5. SSR should be a timed event, without the external demands of writing reports.
6. The teacher may choose to monitor each child using anecdotal records, noting whether the children are engaged in the activity. Disengagement during SSR may indicate that students need help in selecting materials or in other areas of reading development.

At-Home Reading. At-home reading is another important topic to know for the test. The idea is to involve caregivers in the process of helping their children to continue reading when outside of school. Caregivers are probably not teachers, so they need very clear guidelines if at-home reading activities are to succeed (Anderson, 2000). For example, parents need to know that time must be set aside for at-home reading and that signed sheets might be involved to document the process. Also, texts at the child's independent reading level are to be sent home from school to ensure access to materials. A library list might also be developed for the family to assist them in selecting texts for their children.

Involving parents in helping emergent readers to learn CAP is another possibility, if the parents are literate. Parents can be trained in how to model identifying the parts of a book, where to start reading, and so on. The family can also be enlisted in modeling proper intonation patterns and so forth, as described in choral reading. Finally, parents who both speak and read a language other than English can use primary language texts to model CAP (if the language is alphabetic like English), intonation, and even basic comprehension strategies.

General Guidelines for Motivating Students.   Being motivated to read is important because those students who want to read tend to read more than those who find the experience dull and boring. Two sets of guidelines for motivating students to read are used to end this section. The first set contains general classroom considerations; the second set is for students with specific needs in staying motivated to read.

The general classroom guidelines for motivating children to read are as follows (Gambrell, 1985).

1. Provide opportunities for the children to read independently. These opportunities allow children to select and read books for a defined period of time each day, which makes not only the act of reading seem important enough to have time set aside for it, but also provides time for the students to read.
2. Know the interests of the students. Early in the school year, it is important to survey the students to find out what books they want to have in the classroom, the types of magazines, the topics, and so forth. This way, when a child gets the urge to read about something in particular during class, he won't go unsatisfied.
3. Set goals for reading in the classroom. Noncompetitive games can be developed that set goals for the children to read a certain number of books over the course of a month. This can make reading fun, so long as it does not become a situation in which students who need more help are shamed in the process.
4. Include books, magazines, and other reading materials for all of the reading levels in the classroom. No child should be left out of independent reading because books at her reading level are not available.
5. Use the library. Children should be able to find books at the library so that they can use this important resource to find things that they actually want to read for either in-class or at-home reading.

The remaining general guidelines (adapted entirely from the model) are for children who are unmotivated to read.

1. See if the child can decode the text. Decoding problems do not encourage children to read. Provide instruction in this area if it is the major hindrance to reading.
2. If the child can decode, see if the child can comprehend the books that he is reading. Comprehension is addressed in the next section. For now, you can simply understand that if a child cannot understand what he is reading, he probably won't see much point in the process.
3. If both decoding and comprehension are in place, survey the student's interests. Perhaps the literature and topics available to the student in the classroom do not interest her. The only way to know if this is the case is to ask.

4. Set goals for independent-reading level books. Some children may need goals to keep them motivated. Set a number of pages or a number of books from a variety of genres per week. Over time, children are motivated by their progress in reading many books and many types of books.
5. Share books with parents. If the parents are non-English speakers, children's books in the home language can also be used. Bilingual books are especially helpful if the home language is alphabetic and is read in the same direction. In any case, books that the family can enjoy together facilitate this process well.

Having described the critical role that fluency plays in the model and the activities that you should know for its development, the next section discusses reading comprehension. Reading comprehension is the main focus of the reading-to-learn process and includes instruction in vocabulary, comprehension levels, strategies, and text structures.

LEVEL 4: READING COMPREHENSION

This section teaches the elements of reading comprehension instruction that you need to know for the test. In this model, reading comprehension means that the child understands all of the explicit and implied ideas in a text and makes judgments about those ideas.

Here are what the components of reading comprehension look like (Bauman & Schmitt, 1986; Gersten, Fuchs, Williams, & Baker, 2001):

Fluency	Automatic word recognition
Vocabulary development	Structural analysis Using context Building background Elaboration techniques
Comprehension levels	Literal comprehension (answering *who, what, where,* and *when* questions) Inferential comprehension (answering *how* and *why* questions) Evaluative comprehension (making judgments about the text)

Fluency

The first area is fluency and it must be in place before working on higher levels of vocabulary and in each area of comprehension. The last section discussed fluency and how it is developed. If children are not fluent, they do not have enough attention left over to comprehend. This level introduces vocabulary and comprehension, the two most important ingredients in the reading-to-learn process. You need to learn very specific information and particular activities to prepare yourself fully for test questions in this area.

The type of vocabulary at this level of the model requires much deeper strategies that use word structure and sentence and paragraph context to convey meaning. Teaching comprehension requires strategies for literal, inferential, and evaluative comprehension. Text structure also affects how children comprehend what they read, and you need to know activities that address the schema of narrative and expository text.

The first area to explore at the reading comprehension level of the model is vocabulary development.

Vocabulary Development

This section describes advanced vocabulary development. Heavy emphasis and instruction in this area begins when the child decodes text fluently and accurately. For the test, you need to know how to address three essential areas that relate to vocabulary instruction.

1. The challenges that students face when encountering complex vocabulary words
2. The terms associated with upper-level vocabulary instruction
3. The appropriate types of methods that the test values for vocabulary instruction

Each of these areas is described next, beginning with the challenges that students face with learning higher levels of vocabulary.

To understand the challenges that children face when learning upper-elementary vocabulary, you have to know the four types of words that they may encounter in text (Armbruster & Nagy, 1992; Dunn & Graves, 1987).

1. *Words that they know when reading and use in speaking:* These vocabulary words are the most accessible words to children because the meanings "register" when they read them. For example, when they encounter the word *cat* for the first time and decode it, it is likely that they will understand the word if it is already part of their spoken vocabulary. The only real challenge here is to decode the word correctly and comprehend it.
2. *Words that they know in reading but rarely use in speaking:* The most obvious examples of such words are those such as *heretofore* and *aforementioned.* They represent words that we know in reading but probably rarely use in casual conversation. As children read more varieties of text, they develop a reading vocabulary that includes words like these, and the collection may exceed their spoken vocabularies.
3. *Words that they have seen before in only certain spoken or written contexts:* The target vocabulary of developmental activities are the words that students know only in certain contexts and words that are completely unfamiliar to them. For example, a child might say the word *they're* for years but not know it immediately when reading it for the first time in print. Confusions in writing may occur with words such as *site, cite,* and *sight* because the child has only a thin grasp on when to use words such as these in particular contexts.
4. *Words that they have never seen before or used in speech:* Highly specialized vocabulary words from the content areas, such as *entropy,* name concepts that children might not have any clue about. Even its definition as "the second law of thermodynamics" does not help them to understand the word because the concept is totally unfamiliar. So, even if words like these are decoded correctly, they do not conjure up a familiar idea and register meaning. Structurally complex words fall into this category.

In addition to the above areas, you also need to understand how vocabulary activities function and how they are built around the different types of words that students need to learn how to both decode and comprehend. Table 2.12 summarizes these areas.

To ease your study of this important area of the model, the discussion is divided into three parts: before, while, and after vocabulary development activities. Please note that the order of these activities is flexible and that "before" activities could easily be carried out after reading text. This arrangement is meant to simplify your studies only. In reality, these activities are more fluid than their presentation here suggests.

Before-Reading Activities for Vocabulary Development.

Prior Knowledge Activities. Activities that fall into this group ask students to brainstorm and generate words that are related to a topic before it is read and discussed. The following list gives an example of a brainstorming activity on the vocabulary for the topic of "sea life." It exemplifies the knowledge that this model requires you to understand for the test.

TEACHER PREPARATION
1. Prior to introducing a unit on sea life, ask the students to spend five minutes writing down all of the words that they know that relate to ocean animals.
2. Collect all of the responses and write on the board. Ask the students to together extend the lists that they had generated on their own.

TEACHER MODELING
3. Introduce the target vocabulary and any related concepts that are necessary to understand the text that the students will read in this unit (for example, mammals, crustacean, cephalopod, and so on).

GUIDED PRACTICE
4. Have the students group the terms that the class generated in lists under each of the target words.

TABLE 2.12 Vocabulary Activities

BEFORE READING	WHILE READING		POST-READING
Vocabulary Development	*Structural Analysis (Morphology)*		*Using Context*
Prior Knowledge	*Inflectional Suffixes*	*Roots and Derivations*	*Syntax and Semantics*
Association	Plural *-s*	Derivational affixes	Using syntax to gain meaning
Homophones	Possessive *-s*	Root words	Using semantics to gain meaning
Homographs	Third singular *-s*	Base words	Using semantics to gain meaning
Synonyms	Verb tense (*-ed, -ing, -en*)		Thesaurus and dictionary skills
Antonyms	Comparative (*-er, -est*)		
Elaboration			

INDEPENDENT PRACTICE

5. Turn to the text on sea life and have the students read it with these categories in mind.
6. Check for comprehension of the words and the passages through discussions or other means of assessment.

This vocabulary activity makes the unfamiliar become familiar by having the students use their prior knowledge as a bridge to new understandings. A similar activity would ask the students to rate their understanding of the target words first and then read the passage to see if their understandings change as a result of their reading. However, the brainstorming activity on sea life is a far more explicit one that really demonstrates how prior knowledge is used in this model.

Another type of prior knowledge activity is the key word method. In this activity, the teacher simply pulls the vocabulary that she knows will be difficult for most students, develops the words into a list, and selects a variety of activities using the terms. For example, the children can rate their knowledge of each word before learning their definitions prior to reading or as they read the text (Chase & Duffelmeyer, 1990). A simple activity to preteach vocabulary involves having the students imagine the words, use mnemonic devices to remember them, or draw pictures of the definitions of the words.

Association Activities. The brainstorming example on sea life shows how students could generate terms on their own first before relating them to unfamiliar target words. This is the essential feature of association activities, in which known and unknown terms are linked. Many association activities use graphic representations, such as webs and maps, to help students see how the words relate to one another (Rupley, Logan, Nichols, & Nichols, 1998/1999). For example, the teacher and students could create a semantic map on regions of the brain, as shown in Figure 2.11.

The goal is to help students visualize the information and to see how the terms and ideas collected under each part of the map relate to one another (Stahl & Shiel, 1992). As the students read, they could add information to the map. Additionally, other maps could be created to describe the brains of other mammals, fish, and reptiles so that students could see the similarities and differences.

Word Types. Understanding word types helps you to identify activities that assist children in expanding their knowledge of words that sound the same but have different meanings

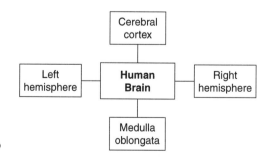

FIGURE 2.11   Semantic Map

(homophones), words that are written the same but have different meanings (homographs), synonyms for words, antonyms for words, and words with multiple meanings.

Following are selected examples of each type of word.

Homophones	site, cite, sight
Homographs	lead (v.) and lead (n.), subject (v.) and subject (n.)
Synonyms	happy, joyful, merry
Antonyms	happy/sad; calm/stressed

Homophones are words that sound the same but their spellings indicate the differences in their meanings and how they are used in sentences. Homographs are words that are written the same way but are pronounced differently. The example in the list gives two sets of words whose meanings change depending on whether the medial vowel is long or short (*lead* v. *lead*) or whether the stress is placed on the first syllable or the second (*subjéct* and *súbject*). Synonyms and antonyms are words that are related to one another either by meaning roughly the same thing or having meanings that are opposite to one another. You need to know activities for words such as these to help children increase their knowledge of such words to increase their comprehension of narrative and expository text. Teaching homophones, homographs, and multiple-meaning words can also be done through semantic features analyses or through graphic representations. However, those activities are pretty hard to describe in the form of an essay. Here is an activity that you could use as a guide for teaching these types of words in elaboration activities (Stahl, 1985).

TEACHER PREPARATION
1. Preselect or create a passage that contains homophones for the students to explore—for example, *cite, site,* and *sight.*
2. Project the passage on a screen for the students.

TEACHER MODELING
3. Highlight two of the homophones on the screen and point out how the spelling affects the meaning of the word.

GUIDED PRACTICE
4. Have the students find other homophones in the text and ask them to use them in sentences that illustrate their meaning—for example, *there, their,* and *they're.*

INDEPENDENT PRACTICE
5. Include these words as part of a homophone word wall that the students could use as part of their in-class writing activities.

Elaboration Activities. Elaboration activities can ask children to compare and contrast the meanings of words. Using lists of words and graphic representations of such words are common ways that teachers instruct children in vocabulary words like these, along with using pictures to provide additional support to communicate the meanings of these words.

Semantic features analyses are another option here. These activities ask students to consider the finer distinctions in the meanings of words (Gifford, 2000). For example, students might be asked to compare the features of words within a particular class of words (Stieglitz & Stieglitz, 1981). Under a large category of *fish* are various types, such as *northern, walleye, perch, bass,* and *trout*. While all of these labels refer to fish, the characteristics of each of them are different. The same is true for many synonyms, such as *sloppy, messy, dirty, disorganized, disarrayed,* and *disheveled*. To learn how to distinguish one term from another, students look at the finer shades of meaning of each of these words. Table 2.13 shows an example (Peregoy & Boyle, 1993).

While-Reading Activities for Vocabulary Development.   *The speaker was condemned for his antidisestablishmentarianism.* A student who encounters *antidisestablishmentarianism* in print for the first time may have trouble comprehending the sentence unless she has been taught to use special skills and strategies to decode and comprehend such a word. Those strategies might involve dividing the word into its open and closed syllables and decoding them. It might look like this (the closed syllables are bracketed):

[an] • ti • [dis] • [es] • ta • [blish] • [ment] • [ar] • i • [an] • [ism]

Given the above, you now can see why phonics instruction ends with open and closed syllable decoding as its last step. An important skill for word analysis is the ability to break the word into syllables first and then to analyze each syllable structurally for its "meaningful" parts (e.g., locating affixes, roots, and base words). (Affixes are things such as prefixes and suffixes: *pre-* and *re-* and *-ment* and *-ion*). Root words are meaningful word parts that build on other words, such as the *ast* in *asteroid* and *asterisk* (*ast* means "star") Base words are those words that can stand by themselves to which prefixes and suffixes attach (for example, *review, worker*).

Table 2.14 shows an example of structural word analysis applied to *antidisestablishmentarianism.*

TABLE 2.13   Shades of Meaning

	DISORGANIZED	DISARRAYED	DISHEVELED
Characterizes a person's behavior	X		
Characterizes a person's appearance			X
Characterizes the order of objects	X	X	
Describes the condition of a location	X	X	

TABLE 2.14   Structural Word Analysis

PREFIX	PREFIX	BASE WORD	SUFFIX	SUFFIX	SUFFIX
anti-	*dis-*	*establish*	*-ment*	*-arian*	*-ism*
Opposed to	the removal of	the state		believers of	a philosophical position

A student would need prior instruction in each of the areas of roots, base words, and affixes to perform the above analysis. The student would then need to learn how to reassemble the word (pronounce it as a whole word, not as individual syllables) and check for its structural meaning against the context of the sentence or paragraph. Roughly, *antidisestablishmentarianism* describes people who are opposed to people who adhere to a belief of removing a governing body. Phew. In the upper grades, students need a variety of strategies like the one for this word and for other types of words that they encounter in text.

Before explaining the methods for vocabulary that you need to know for the test, you need to have a quick review of morphology and other terms associated with vocabulary instruction.

Morphology for Structural Analysis. Structural analysis was used to analyze the *morphology* of the word *antidisestablishmentarianism,* and it is an important strategy used to decode and comprehend polysyllabic, content-area words. For you to fully understand how structural analysis works, you need to have some understanding of the following terms: *morphemes, inflections,* and *derivations.* Morphemes are important aspects of structural analysis since they are the smallest meaningful units of a word. For example, the word *cat* has three letters in it: *c, a, t.* It also has three sounds: /k/, /a/, /t/. Together, these sounds and letters represent one morpheme, even though it has three letters and three sounds. This is because the sounds and the letters come together to make one meaningful unit; thus, there is one morpheme.

The word *cats* is another story. It contains two morphemes. Here is how it works. The three letters that form *cat* form one morpheme; and the plural marker *-s* represents the second morpheme. So, there are two morphemes here: *cat* plus *s.* To make sure that you understand how this works, consider the combination of letters *ptfs. Ptfs* represents no morphemes. This is because this combination of letters means absolutely nothing in English. Recognize also that many polysyllabic words cannot be analyzed structurally, either. For example, though *chimpanzee* can be divided into syllables, it cannot be analyzed to find its "meaningful parts." It doesn't have any, unless all of the letters and syllables are combined to make one morpheme.

Besides the collection of letters that make meaningful words, as in *cat* and *dog,* there are very special kinds of morphemes that we divide into two groups. The first group of special morphemes are called inflections, and the second special group is called derivations (Wysock & Jenkins, 1987).

Inflectional suffixes make plurals, possessives, comparatives, and verb tenses, but do not change a word from a noun to a verb or an adjective to an adverb. Since you might need some examples of each kind of inflection, here is a list to help you out.

Plurals	books, cars, wishes
Possessives	Mike's, Chris's
comparative	bigger (comparative), biggest (superlative)
Verb tenses	walks, walked, walking

The morpheme *s* is very special. It makes plurals (books, cars, wishes), possessives (Mike's, Chris's), and the third-person singular form of many verbs (he walks, she runs). A special feature of the morpheme *s* is its sounds. Say the words from the plurals list aloud to yourself (*books, cars, wishes*). You should notice that the *s* has three different sounds. In *books,* it sounds like the *s* in *see;* in *cars,* it sounds like the *z* in *zoo;* finally, in *wishes,* it sounds like /ez/. What's going on?

These three sounds associated with this inflectional suffixes are called allophones. The environments in which *s* finds itself make it sound like either an /s/ or /z/ or an /ez/. Here is why. *Books* ends with the letter *k* while *cars* ends with the letter *r.* Put your hand on your throat and say the words *book* and *car* to yourself a few times. You should notice that your throat doesn't vibrate when you say the letter *k* but it does when you say the letter *r.* This is because *k* is unvoiced, while *r* is voiced: when *s* follows an unvoiced letter, it sounds like /s/; when *s* follows a voiced letter, it sounds like /z/. And when *s* follows the letters *sh* or *ch* (for example, *wishes* and *churches*), it always sounds like /ez/.

Inflections are typically taught early since they are an important part of decoding simple words. Plurals, possessives, and tense markers are taught as units to be decoded, with little to no emphasis on the terminology. Common techniques in the early grades to teach inflections include using pocket charts to attach inflectional endings to familiar words, (for example, to change *dog* to *dogs* and *cat* to *cats*). These activities can grow more complex as the spellings of some base words to which inflectional endings are attached may change. For example, some letters are dropped or doubled when adding *-ed* and *-ing* (for example, *drop—dropped; run—running*).

Word Study for Inflectional Morphology. Word study activities can also serve this purpose. Students write words according to the allophones heard in plurals, possessives, and third-singular verbs. Following are examples:

/s/	*slips, tricks, hits*
/z/	*runs, ties, buys*
/ez/	*washes, churches*

The reason that it is important for you to know about these aspects of inflections is that you just might be asked to identify inflectional endings, or allophones, or to diagnose a child's spelling of the word *cars* as *carz.* Furthermore, the other inflections, including the possessives, the comparatives (*-er* and the superlative *-est*), and the verb tenses might be part of lesson plans that you have to describe or multiple-choice questions that you have to answer. Knowing how inflections work will be very helpful to you on the exam.

Structural Analysis for Derivational Activities. The next activity teaches students to use structural analysis skills when they encounter words in text to broaden their vocabularies and aid their comprehension (White, Power, & White, 1989). Here, students learn explicit methods to pick words apart into their roots, bases, and affixes while they are reading.

Activities for derivations begin by teaching students to understand the terms *prefix, suffix, base word,* and *root word.* The following is an activity that illustrates how to accomplish this goal (Burns, Roe, & Ross, 1999; White & Yanagihara, 1989; and, O'Grady et al., 1993).

TEACHER PREPARATION

1. Teach the derivational affix terms *prefix* and *suffix* and how a prefix can change a word's meaning and how a suffix can change a word from a noun to an adjective, an adjective to a verb, and a verb to a noun.

TEACHER MODELING

2. Write the word *denationalization* on the board.
3. Underline the base word.

de<u>nation</u>alization

GUIDED PRACTICE

4. Separate the derivational affixes (prefixes and suffixes) in the word:

de <u>nation</u> **al iz ation**

5. Show how the prefix *de* and suffixes *al, iz,* and *ation* affect the meaning and the grammatical category of the word:

de	<u>nation</u>	**al**	**iz**	**ation**
|	|	|	|	|
"Un"	noun	adjective	verb	noun

INDEPENDENT PRACTICE

6. Have students find other words in their reading that are made up of derivational affixes like prefixes and suffixes and have them show how these elements can change both the meaning and the grammatical categories of a word.

The second type of structural analysis moves beyond teaching categories such as prefix and suffix. In these activities, students learn how to apply techniques directly to their readings. The following is an activity that explicitly teaches Greek and Latin roots (Gunning, 2003; Vacca et al., 2003).

TEACHER MODELING

1. Model ways that Greek and Latin roots make up many words that we know—for example, that *tele* is a Greek root that is found in many common words (for example, *telephone, television, telescope*).
2. Teach the meaning of the root word (for example, *tele* means "to send").
3. Teach several Greek and Latin roots and write them on the board (for example, *ast* means *star*).

GUIDED PRACTICE

4. Ask students to generate as many words as possible that use this root for their meaning (for example, *asteroid, asterisk*).

INDEPENDENT PRACTICE

5. Have the students search their text for these and other roots and list them in their reading logs.

6. Develop classroom charts that collect words under headings that contain Greek and Latin roots that the children have learned.
7. Read a text in which other root words are used and check for understanding.

These activities teach students skills that students should use actively when they encounter unfamiliar words. Much like decoding, the students should use their powers of deduction explicitly to analyze words and uncover their meanings.

Post-Reading Activities for Vocabulary Development.   The final area is using context either while or after reading (Carr, Dewitz, & Patberg, 1989). According to this model, children must learn how to use the grammar of the English language (*syntax*) and the meaning of words in sentences and paragraphs (*semantics*) to understand what they are reading. To illustrate this point, think about the following sentence:

I _____ the book.

If you were to list the words that could fit in the blank, most likely you would generate words such as *like, liked, buy, bought, have, had,* or *returned.* What you might not immediately recognize is that these words are all verbs. Your list would not include color words, such as *orange* or *blue,* or nouns, such as *building* or *automobile.* This is because you have internalized the grammar of the English language and unconsciously know that only verbs can fit that space. You apply English syntax to your reading. Students learning to use context to understand unfamiliar words need this skill, too.

Semantics affects vocabulary in the following way. If we add *yesterday* to the example sentence, the possible words from our list are reduced.

I _____ the book yesterday.

Adding *yesterday* to the sentence immediately eliminates several words from our sentence: *like, buy, have.* The semantics of *yesterday* affects the syntax of our possible verbs because all of them now must appear in the past tense. Furthermore, if we add even more semantic information, we reduce our list to one possibility.

I _____ the book yesterday; it was expensive.

The only possible word now that fits into the sentence is the word *bought.* Because we use syntax and semantics when we read, we can figure out which words are possible in sentences and which ones make the most sense when we read.

What children must learn about context is how to use syntactic and semantic information when reading. This helps them to figure out the meanings of words when they encounter them in sentences, whether they are familiar with them or not. The word *antidisestablishmentarianism* can be analyzed structurally for its meaning, but then the child might have to analyze the surrounding context in which the word is used to confirm what it means within the sentence, based on its position in the sentence and on other words and sentences that surround it.

The same idea is true for homophones, homographs, and words with multiple meanings. Take the word *hammer,* for example. It is far more commonly used than is *antidis-*

establishmentarianism, but children may still have to use syntax and semantics to figure out its meaning from context.

1. I hammered the nail.
2. The baseball player hammered a home run.
3. That driver seems to be hammered since he can't drive straight.

While *hammered* appears syntactically as a verb in each of the sentences above, it does not carry the same meaning. The syntax and semantics of each of the words changes depending on the context in which it is used. In short, students need to learn how to use context to understand even familiar words that they encounter in print, or they risk carrying very different and potentially incorrect notions away from what they have read. Note that context is always last in this model because it is seen as an unreliable predictor of word meaning; knowing the word in isolation and being able to reach its meaning through analyzing its morphology are favored here.

Activities for Using Context.   Using context is viewed as a very elusive ability for students to acquire. As a matter of fact, context is almost nonexistent during early reading because it is thought to distract and interfere with decoding instruction. For some, even pictures that accompany text are thought to be a detriment because they might supply "too much context" and take away from a student's relying on print as the sole means for developing decoding skills (Groff, 1998).

At higher levels of vocabulary instruction in the upper grades, context is an important part of confirming the meanings of words, after the student has tried to attack the word using prior knowledge and structural analyses. Context is almost a secondary consideration because it is thought to be an unreliable means of uncovering the meanings of unfamiliar words with any consistency (Schatz, 1986).

Context, as a supporting element, is viewed as useful in activities designed to preteach unfamiliar words (Schefelbine, 1990). The following is an activity that is common for teaching students to use context to figure out the meanings of unfamiliar words (Gifford, 2000; Nagy, 1998; Townsend & Clarihew, 1989).

TEACHER PREPARATION
1. Isolate words that may be unfamiliar to students (for example, words that are highly irregular and not immediately recognizable from print or context).
2. Write the words on the board (for example, *effete, morose, hebetudinous*) and ask students for definitions.

TEACHER MODELING
3. Build sentences around the words on the board (for example, "You could tell that the audience members found the speaker to be very *hebetudinous* since they were fast asleep at the end of his speech").

GUIDED PRACTICE
4. Ask the students to generate familiar words that could replace the unknown word (for example, *dull, boring*).

INDEPENDENT PRACTICE

5. Reveal the meanings of the words to the class or have the students use dictionaries to confirm whether their use of context was effective.

6. Apply strategy within the context of reading on preselected passages that will yield positive results for the students.

One classroom activity that can cover all types of vocabulary words, from basic sight words and decodable words to content area and derivational words, is the word wall. Henning and Pickett (2000) describe three types of word walls for high-frequency words, words from literature, and words from the social and biological sciences. As students encounter new and unfamiliar words (or as the teacher preplans such encounters), words are written on index cards and placed on the wall at the front of the room under their alphabetic category. The words are then used as the basis for games, as inclusions in journal writing, or as reference words during discussions. This way, the students can see the words each day and use them until they become part of their spoken vocabularies. Figure 2.12 shows a word wall for some of the words encountered in this chapter.

Having described the role vocabulary plays in comprehension and the activities that accompany it, the next section turns to comprehension itself to explore how it is viewed and instructed in this model.

FIGURE 2.12   Word Wall

A affix alphabetic principle allophone	B blend	C conventional	D derivation digraph	E elementary expository
F	G graphophonic	H	I inferential IRI	J
K	L literal comprehension	M magic score miscue morphology	N	O onset
P phonemic awareness phonics	Q	R rime running record	S syllable syntax	T transitional
U	V visual	W word wall	X	Y/Z

Reading Comprehension (Literal, Inferential, and Evaluative)

There are three areas of comprehension that you have to know for the test.

1. The three levels of comprehension: literal, inferential, and evaluative
2. The strategies associated with teaching comprehension skills
3. The role that text organization plays in reading comprehension

There are also activities that pertain to narrative and expository text exclusively. These are explained last.

This model of reading instruction divides comprehension into three distinct categories that you should know for the test: literal comprehension, inferential comprehension, and evaluative comprehension. There are different levels of questions that are associated with each comprehension category, which are shown in Table 2.15.

Literal Comprehension.   Literal comprehension is about identifying factual ideas that are explicitly stated in a given text. This often involves answering *who, what, where,* and *when* questions after reading a passage. Both narrative stories and informational essays can be analyzed through these questions. For example, in a simple adventure story, you can ask who the main characters are, what they are doing, and where they are going. Similarly, informational texts can be analyzed this way since it is possible to answer questions about who a historical figure is, what she accomplished, where she lived, and when her defining moment occurred. Literal comprehension means that students capture all of the factual and explicitly stated ideas in a text on their own. Questions associated with this level of understanding are viewed as being of a lower order since they ask students to recall basic facts that are presented in the text or to translate information from the text into simple oral or written responses to factually based questions.

TABLE 2.15   Reading Comprehension

LITERAL COMPREHENSION	INFERENTIAL COMPREHENSION	EVALUATION OF TEXT
Identifying explicit main ideas, details, sequences, cause-effect, patterns	Identifying implicit main ideas, details, comparisons, cause-effect Drawing conclusions Making predictions	Recognizing bias Distinguishing fact from opinion
Memory questions Recall information Translate or change information	Interpretation questions interpret relationships among facts Apply facts to new contexts	Higher-order questions Analyze new situations with new knowledge Synthesize information among texts Evaluate the text

Inferential Comprehension.   Inferential comprehension is about uncovering ideas that are only implied in a text (Carr, 1983). Answering *how* and *why* questions best illustrate this level of comprehension. *How* and *why* questions can be applied to either narrative or expository text to reveal ideas that are not explicitly stated. When children read and understand stories literally, they can then learn how to read beyond the words on the page to try to understand *why* characters behave and think as they do. Informational texts can also be read this way. Children might be asked to extend their understanding of an informational text beyond the facts, such as when they are asked to propose how a problem such as global warming can be solved, even if the piece did not offer any solutions.

Inferential comprehension questions ask students to think beyond the facts of the text. Questions associated with this area of comprehension are thought to be of a higher order because the student must read for understandings that are not explicitly stated. Questions that ask the student to interpret information in the text or to apply these facts in some way typify these types of questions.

Evaluative Comprehension.   This model places evaluative comprehension at the highest level. It requires students to make judgments about texts and to base these assessments on what they have understood both literally and inferentially. This also means that students have to learn how to tell fact from opinion and to identify propaganda when they read it. Making these distinctions helps them to make qualified evaluations of the relative worth (or lack of worth) of a given text that they have read and understood. These types of questions move beyond *who, what, where, why,* and *when* into the realm of belief and disbelief, support or opposition, and fact or opinion.

In sum, literal comprehension is about factual understanding; inferential comprehension is about understanding implied meanings; and evaluative comprehension is about making objective and subjective judgments about what was read. This model also suggests that a hierarchy exists that affects the way you are to teach each of these components of comprehension. Literal comprehension precedes inferential comprehension and inferential comprehension precedes evaluative comprehension (Hansen & Pearson, 1983). Here is why.

The literal understandings that children take away from a text regarding *who, what, where,* and *when* the story takes place form the basis for answering *how* and *why* questions. In short, answering inferential comprehension questions is not possible unless the child can grasp the most basic factual elements of the story. Furthermore, the student cannot be expected to make effective judgments about a story without having first understood the text's explicit and implied meanings.

Activities for comprehension are sensitive to these assumptions. The first group of strategies develops a student's prior knowledge before reading a text, helps the student self-regulate understanding while he reads the text, and teaches the student to extend the knowledge beyond the text after it has been read.

Comprehension Strategies.   Comprehension strategies are divided into three categories. Prereading strategies occur before the text is read and help students to figure out what they know before reading and to inspire interest. Students then learn to apply while-reading strategies to check understanding, repair misunderstandings, and keep working through a text (Pressley, Brown, Beard El-Dinary, & Afflerbach, 1995). These strategies occur as the student is reading. The final group of strategies occurs after the child has read. Here, they learn to con-

TABLE 2.16 Comprehension Strategies and Activities

Prereading	Prereading strategies	*Anticipation guides* *KWL activities* *Brainstorming*
While-reading	Metacognitive strategies	*Think alouds* *Story maps*
After-reading	Elaboration strategies	*Perspectives for narrative and expository text*

nect what they have understood to other texts and to make evaluative judgments about what they have read. Table 2.16 shows these activities and their characteristics (Dowhower, 1999).

Prereading Activities. Prereading activities help students to access prior knowledge (concepts and ideas with which they are already familiar) and to develop interest in what they are going to read (Langer, 1981). These strategies can also help the students to recognize gaps or identify misunderstandings in their knowledge about a subject that is filled in or changed during the reading. Identifying prior knowledge helps them to comprehend unfamiliar ideas. The activities that exemplify prereading strategies are anticipation guides and Know-Want-Learned (KWL) activities, both of which can be adapted and applied to either narrative or expository text. Other types of brainstorming activities are also possible. Anticipation guides are described first.

ANTICIPATION GUIDES

■ Anticipation guides (Duffelmeyer, 1994; Duffelmeyer & Baum, 1992) can be used as prereading activities that teachers develop to help students rate their understanding of a subject before they try to read it. These guides are explicit and ask direct questions for the students to rate, which not only tests their current understandings but also cues them for what to look for as they read a text. These responses are checked against their understanding after they have read the text during post-reading activities.

The general steps are as follows (Ausubel, 1963; Newell, 1984).

TEACHER PREPARATION
1. Review a passage and identify statements in the passage that students can rate prior to reading.
2. Develop a balance of questions that may confirm or challenge their present understandings. For example, "Whales, like humans, are mammals. True or False."
3. Rate the items as either true or false or as a self-assessment. For example, "I think I know it" or "I don't think I know it."

TEACHER MODELING
4. Have students read and mark each statement as true or false as they read.

GUIDED PRACTICE
5. Work with students to confirm or deny several questions before having them work independently.

INDEPENDENT PRACTICE

6. After having read the passage, students compare what they thought prior to reading and what they know after they have read it.

KWL ACTIVITIES

■ KWL activities (Carr & Ogle, 1987) help students to access prior knowledge and to set their own goals for reading, which helps them to sustain interest in the topic since they are attempting to answer their own questions. KWL is an acronym for *what* we know, what we *want* to know, and what we have *learned* (Ogle, 1986). These questions are used as column headings on worksheets. Students complete the first two columns prior to reading. The third column is completed after the students have read the text. Here is what a KWL worksheet looks like (Bryan, 1998).

KWL FOR PHONEMIC AWARENESS

Know	Want to know	Learned
Phonemic awareness is for sound instruction.	Why is sound instruction important? How are sounds taught?	(Completed later)

The first column is used to collect all the ideas that students have about a subject. Typically, the teacher introduces the topic to the students and asks them to list their ideas on a separate sheet of paper. These responses are then collected on the board so that a whole-class representation is in front of them. These responses are then added to the "know" column. Students use those responses to generate questions about what they want to know, which are written in the "want to know" column.

When students read the material, they try to see if their prior knowledge is correct and whether the text answers any of the questions they have posed. After they finish reading, confirm statements, and answer questions, the teacher discusses the text, statements, and answers with the class. Students fill in the "what we have learned" column after this discussion to note any changes in what they thought they knew and what they wanted to learn.

While-Reading Activities.   Self-regulation while reading (also termed *metacognition*) is an important part of the model, and this skill is taught explicitly until it becomes internalized (Herrman, 1988). In this view, the reader needs to monitor understanding as the text is read. For example, readers need strategies to maintain motivation and comprehension, to repair misunderstandings, and to untangle confusions. If the reader does not possess strategies for each of these areas, she may give up when she becomes confused or leave the reading with only a partial understanding.

While-reading strategies can be taught individually or in small-group settings with students who share the same need. A full discussion of small and individual instruction models takes place later in this chapter. The structure of the activities is similar to all of the "skills-to-strategies" methods explored so far: The teacher models the skill, the teacher and student practice together, and the student practices independently (Kucan & Beck, 1997). Remedial instruction occurs until the student has internalized the strategy and can perform it without assistance.

The activity that is generalized most easily to the test is the think-aloud activity because it incorporates metacognitive self-regulation, checking for understanding, and repairing that the child needs to internalize. As its name implies, the activity asks students to learn how to "talk their way" through the more challenging aspects of a story or informational text. Imagine that a student reads a passage aloud with good accuracy and fluency, but then performs poorly on literal and inferential comprehension questions. The student might need to acquire strategies to use as he reads the text that direct his attention toward comprehension.

The steps for a think-aloud activity are as follows (Babbs & Moe, 1983; Bauman, Seifert, Kessel, & Jones, 1992).

INITIAL ASSESSMENT
1. Have the student read the passage silently first to ensure that the child is not focusing on performance, which might take away from comprehension.
2. Ask the literal and inferential comprehension questions. If the answers demonstrate continued needs in comprehension, teach the child strategies to maintain comprehension.

TEACHER MODELING
3. Read the passage aloud to the student as she follows along.
4. Model self-questioning strategies by asking comprehension questions aloud and using the text to answer them (*Who are the main characters? Where are they? What are they going to do? Why are they going? How does the story end?*).

GUIDED PRACTICE
5. Practice modeling these same questions with the students on the same passage.

INDEPENDENT PRACTICE
6. Have the students practice this strategy on a new passage and note performance.

Story maps are another viable option for while-reading activities since they can be created as the child reads a story. See the section on graph organizations in this chapter for more information on creating story maps.

Post-Reading Activities.   Post-reading activities help students extend the knowledge that they have acquired from a passage to new texts or situations. They also help students to compare and contrast texts, authors, genres, and so on. Obviously, students have to have understood each text both literally and inferentially to accomplish this rather daunting goal. Before presenting specific activities for narrative and expository text, the text shows you a simple set of steps that illustrate typical post-reading activities.

Perspective activities are common activities that help students to read beyond the text and to evaluate the merits and shortcomings of the content (Cioffi, 1992). Expository text, for example, often presents information that affects people in positive and negative ways. Perspective activities help students to recognize this and to learn how to judge positions, gain empathy, and make decisions. They also learn how to separate fact from opinion when making choices that affect others and themselves.

The following activity illustrates an elaboration activity for expository text (Maria, 1990; Vacca & Vacca, 1989).

TEACHER PREPARATION

1. Select a passage of expository text that presents a problem that affects different groups of people in a variety of ways (for example, the benefits and detriments of sending an industry from a small Midwestern town to another country where the labor is cheaper and the environmental regulations are lax).
2. Ensure that the students have understood the material both literally and inferentially.

TEACHER MODELING

3. Use a whole-class activity to brainstorm and list ideas about all of the people who might be affected by the information that is presented in the text.
4. Group students and assign positions for them to take (for example, as workers, managers, city planners from the town and overseas).

GUIDED PRACTICE

5. Have the students develop responses for each point of view and use the text to support their positions for what is the "right thing to do." Teach the students to separate facts (that is, ideas supported with measurable evidence) from opinions (that is, ideas supported by emotions) when supporting their positions.

CHECK COMPREHENSION

6. Bring the groups together again and ask them to present their positions on the issues raised by the text and how they will affect people in the text.

This activity illustrates how an elaboration activity asks students to move beyond literal and inferential comprehension to learn how to evaluate positions and separate fact from opinion when developing an argument.

Strategies for comprehension are useful for pre-, while-, and after-reading to help students to access prior knowledge, check and repair understandings and misunderstandings, and elaborate knowledge after they have read a story. The next essential ingredient that you must learn about is the role that the structure of the text plays in comprehension. Narrative and expository text are organized in different ways that may affect the children's ability to comprehend what they read, regardless of the strategies that they employ (Gersten, Fuchs, Williams, & Baker, 2001). You need to learn explicit methods to teach children to use the structure of the text to understand what they read, along with the strategies for comprehension just reviewed.

Reading Comprehension and Text Organization (Schemata).   In this model, text organization is an important consideration because there is a hierarchy associated with which type of text is taught first and which is taught last. Since young children are probably more accustomed to hearing and following stories from a young age, it is thought they probably internalize a great deal of the elements of a story, such as plot, setting, and characters. When they hear and begin to read stories independently, they know what to expect in these areas. The teacher's task is to begin teaching the students how to understand narrative text literally and inferentially, based on their prior knowledge of stories.

Expository text, on the other hand, is viewed differently. Since the organizational patterns of this type of text are different, even more explicit instruction might be required. For example, it is possible for a child to read an essay about sea life and not understand it because he is reading it for its story elements and not its details. The child goes into the reading with the idea that he is going to encounter main characters, problems, and resolutions, but what he finds instead are facts, figures, tables, and so on. Since the reader lacks experience with this type of textual organization, he does not know how to overcome the disconnection between narrative and expository text.

For the exam, you have to understand comprehension in the terms just described. To review briefly, there are three different types of comprehension that you have to know: including literal, inferential, and evaluative. This is also the order of instruction and expectation. Furthermore, the type of text and its organizational pattern has an impact on what the students understand literally and inferentially. Finally, expository text might require more explicit instruction to avoid information breakdowns since its structure is not as familiar as that of narrative text.

Schemata Activities for Narrative Text. The schema associated with narrative text includes the structure of stories (for example, setting, major problem, rising action, climax, resolution), story elements (for example, characters), and literary devices (for example, symbol, metaphor, theme, foreshadowing, imagery). To be able to comprehend text literally and inferentially, and to be able to evaluate it, students must be able to understand all of the common things included in stories.

Graphic organizers that represent all of the elements of a story in a visual way are very common. Typically, the graphic organizer presents descriptive answers to questions associated with the structure of a story that the students have read. Figure 2.13 shows a common graphic organizer called a story map (Shanahan & Shanahan, 1997).

The questions in the diagram can be expanded to include much deeper questions about plot, setting, and character. In addition, portions of the graphic can be highlighted as the student reads the story and the answers can be collected on the chart and then transposed into a reading log or journal.

Graphic organizers can become far more complex than this example (Merkley & Jefferies, 2000/2001; Rakes, Rakes, & Smith, 1995). They can also be used to represent literary devices such as symbol and metaphor (Au & Scheu, 1989). The next example is from Ernest Hemingway's *The Old Man and the Sea.* For those of you who have not read the story in a while, missed it somehow, or avoided it on purpose, here is a brief synopsis.

An old man gets in a small boat and goes fishing on the ocean for what might be his last trip (he's pretty old, remember). He catches the fish of a lifetime and spends many pages bringing

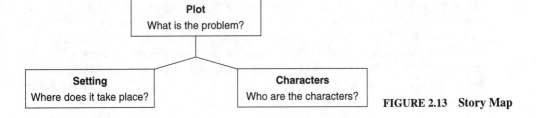

FIGURE 2.13   Story Map

it in. It is so big that he has keep it next to the boat. As he returns home, his prize fish is attacked and destroyed by sharks. All that is left of his wonderful fish is the skeleton. The old man sails one way and the skeleton floats to another part of the island. Later, the skeleton washes on shore and some tourists see it. They comment that a storm must have killed the fish.

A graphic organizer can be used to teach the symbol and metaphor present in the story. Following is an example applied to this story (DiCecco & Gleason, 2002).

1. After reading the story *The Old Man and the Sea* and ensuring that the students have understood it literally and inferentially, teach symbol and metaphor. Symbol is a thing that represents something else outside of the story, and metaphor is an implied comparison between the story itself and real life.

2. Use a graphic organizer to represent the structure of the story and its other elements:

Old Man *catches the* **Fish** *is attacked by* **Sharks** *leave the* **Bones** *that* **Tourists** *see*

3. Ask students to think about what each of the story's elements could symbolize and create a diagram to illustrate the relationships:

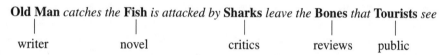

4. Ask the students to think about what the story could represent metaphorically and provide opportunities for discussion. For example, the story might be saying that the public does not see the struggles that writers go through to create their novels; all that they see are the remnants of the critique.

In sum, graphic organizers help students see the structure of stories visually. These structures can be as basic as questions related to plot, setting, and character, or as complex as symbol and metaphor. Use this example to identify questions about how graphic organizers are used to promote literacy or to answer questions about what purpose a particular graphic organizer is serving from a data set with an example.

Analyzing Narrative Text Schema.   Let's look at the activities associated with each area of comprehending narrative text.

IMAGERY ACTIVITIES

■ Imagery activities are teacher-directed activities. A teacher instructs students in ways to create concrete images of important descriptions in a text. Often, descriptions of the setting foreshadow events or reveal problems that are unspoken within the text. For example, in Edgar Allan Poe's *The Fall of the House of Usher,* the text offers a lengthy and rich description of the Usher home, complete with its gloomy exterior, its overgrown foliage, and so on. A critical and foretelling element in the description is a crack that runs down the length of the home to its foundation, which represents an underlying flaw in the family. It might be easy for students to overlook such an element in the description, unless they are shown ways to look for and read for such things.

An imagery activity can help students to understand the role that descriptions play in literature. The following steps characterize these activities (Irwin, 1991).

TEACHER PREPARATION
1. Select important passages that can be analyzed for foreshadowing or other literary devices.

TEACHER MODELING
2. Read the selections aloud to the students and have them use their imaginations to create mental representations of the descriptions and to include as many details as possible.

GUIDED PRACTICE
3. Ask the students to write down impressions about what the descriptions are suggesting about what might happen next in the story.
4. Read the story together to confirm those predictions to see how the descriptions and events relate to one another.
5. Return to whole-group activity to confirm or deny predictions as a class.

INDEPENDENT PRACTICE
6. Have students select other descriptive passages and practice this activity independently.

CHARACTER ANALYSES

■ Character analyses help students see relationships between what characters say and then what they actually do in the story. These relationships can reveal important motivations and contradictions and shed light on whether characters are protagonists, antagonists, or somewhere in the middle. The following steps characterize a character analysis activity.

TEACHER PREPARATION
1. Select key quotations, asides, or thoughts that characters express and events in a story that are related and reveal something important to the reader about the character's true self.

TEACHER MODELING AND GUIDED PRACTICE
2. Read the selections to the students (or have them read them independently).
3. Present the events to the students and discuss how the character's statements relate to one another. For example, in *A Separate Peace* by John Knowles, the narrator goes to great lengths to describe his admiration for one of the other major characters in the story. Later, the narrator is involved in an accident that cripples this friend. The reader is left to decide whether the accident was truly an accident or a deliberate act of jealousy. Comparing statements with events could shed light on what happened and why.

INDEPENDENT PRACTICE
4. Have the students practice this technique independently on other events, comparing what happened with what had been said.

Responding to Narrative Text Schemata.   To help children elaborate and extend their understandings of what they read, children use discussion journals and learning logs. These instruments transfer easily to the test.

DISCUSSION JOURNALS

■ Discussion journals offer students opportunities to interact with the text (Hancock, 1992) or to interact with the teacher about the text in writing (Gambrell, 1985). A typical method for enabling this interaction is to divide sections down the middle. On one side of the page, passages are copied from the text with their page numbers and references. On the other side, the student writes personal responses to or analyses of the quotes. They can also be used for learning strategies, as Table 2.17 shows. The teacher collects the journals and reads the entries. When the teacher comments, she considers the student, the student's response, and the text. Virtually all of the activities described in this section can be conducted this way. Think-aloud entries, prereading entries, and graphic organizers offer opportunities for the teacher and student to carry out written discussions with one another, which helps students learn how to respond to what they are reading.

Schemata Activities for Expository Text.   Graphic organizers can be used to illustrate all of the organizational patterns for expository text. These patterns include detailed descriptions, sequences, comparisons, causes and effects, and problems and solutions. Each type of pattern has schematics that students can fill in as they read, so that they can see the relationships clearly before them (Baxendell, 2003; Irwin, 1991). Figure 2.14 shows such options.

TABLE 2.17   Learning Strategies

MY IMPRESSIONS	MS. BAILEY
At first, I wasn't sure what the word *obsequious* meant in the sentence. I tried to divide it up into syllables, but that didn't work. Finally, I had to use the dictionary to get the meaning.	That's a good use of strategies! Not all of them will work the first time. The most important thing is that you didn't give up. Instead, you used a resource to figure out the meaning of the word. Next time, you might also try to use the context of the sentence first before you check the definition. You might find that you can trust your instincts more often than you think.

Details	Sequences	Comparisons	Cause/Effect	Problem/Solution

FIGURE 2.14   Expository Text Schematic

The students learn each of these patterns and then receive instruction in how to fill them in as they read to help them to visualize details in the story and the relationships among them. These details and relationships might otherwise be overlooked because they are abstract.

SURVEY, QUESTION, READ, RECITE, REVIEW (SQ3R)

■ Another typical activity uses the structure of expository text itself to teach the schema called SQ3R. SQ3R is an acronym for *survey, question, read, recite, review.* Each part of the acronym asks students to perform specific actions with the text (Tadlock, 1978). These actions help students learn about how the information is organized in the passage, making it more understandable.

Here is each step in the SQ3R process (Adamson, 1993).

1. Survey: Students skim and scan the text to get the gist of what it is about.
2. Question: Students read each of the headings in an expository text and turn it into a question. For example, the heading "The Essential Components of Phonemic Awareness" becomes, "What are the essential components of phonemic awareness?" These questions can be written on the text (if it is a copy) or into the learning log.
3. Read: Students read the passage carefully with the questions that they generated from the headings firmly in mind.
4. Recite: After reading, students attempt to answer the questions that they generated from memory, either by saying the answers to themselves or writing them down in their learning logs.
5. Review: The students then check their answers against the text and make changes as required.

This activity uses the structure passage itself as a tool for learning. The headings are converted to study questions and the details are used to answer them.

QUESTION-ANSWER RELATIONSHIP

■ Question-answer relationships (QARs) are helpful for the test since they help students answer questions based on information found within and beyond the text. Often, students need explicit instruction in learning how to answer the questions that accompany expository text. This activity accomplishes this task.

There are four categories of questions that are taught in this activity. They range from low-level memory questions to higher-level evaluation questions (McIntosh & Draper, 1995; Mesmer & Hutchins, 2002; Raphael, 1982):

1. Right there: The answer is found in specific areas of the text.
2. Think and search: The answer is found by assembling several pieces of the text together.
3. Author and me: The answer requires an interpretation of the author's point of view and your own.
4. On my own: The answer comes from the reader's own perspective on what the text advocates.

Each of these questions are applied to the passage that follows to illustrate how they help students learn to answer expository text questions.

> Phonemic awareness is the foundation of decoding instruction. Within this area are four important areas to know. These areas are identifying sounds, discriminating sounds, blending sounds, and segmenting sounds. Segmenting sounds is the highest skill that shows that the child is ready to begin phonics instruction because it indicates that the child can break spoken words into sounds that can be later attached to letters.
>
> Instruction in sounds is not without controversy. Though phonemic awareness is seen as an important predictor of a child's ability to read, this point of view is taken because students who can't read in the upper grades have trouble with phonemic awareness activities. But what if these abilities are only a by-product of being able to read and not a central factor at all?
>
> 1. What is phonemic awareness?
> 2. Which element of phonemic awareness is most important and why?
> 3. What do critics of phonemic awareness instruction have to say?
> 4. What do you think about early phonemic awareness instruction and later reading achievement?

Each of these questions moves from "right there" to "on my own." Instructing QAR relies on explicit instruction in the beginning, where students read the questions first and then turn to the text to highlight the parts of the passage that either provide the answer directly or offer some guidance for a student's own thoughts. This method is then applied to other passages, until students can automatically use QAR as a means of answering after-reading questions.

Study Skills for Expository Text Schemata.   You are also expected to understand how to assess and to teach study skills to students, especially for expository text comprehension (its structure lends itself to such endeavors). Assessments look primarily at the areas of whether the child can interpret tables and diagrams, locate information in a text through skimming and scanning, and identify reference materials (Rogers, 1984). Such assessments can be performed through worksheets or hands-on activities that the teacher observes.

Study skills activities follow the same pattern established in the assessments. Many of the these activities have clever names like PLAN (Caverly, Mandeville, & Nicholson, 1995), which is an acronym for *predict, locate, add,* and *note.* This activity uses visual maps, note taking, and summary writing to help students use the text to prepare for tests. The features that all study skills activities share include activating prior knowledge, retrieving information, taking notes, and writing summaries. If you are asked questions about teaching these skills, you should try to find items that cover all of these elements.

STUDY SYSTEMS

■ The following activity helps prepare you to answer essay questions about how to teach these skills (Palincsar & Brown, 1986; Simpson et al., 1988).

TEACHER PREPARATION

1. Have students use aspects of KWL to find out what they already know about the topic and what they want to find out.
2. Use SQ3R to skim the text and to draw questions out from the text.

GUIDED PRACTICE

3. Show the students how to capture the headings from the text in a graphic organizer to illustrate the relationships among the major ideas.

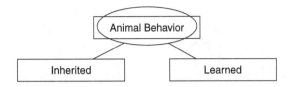

INDEPENDENT PRACTICE

4. Ask the students to read the text and to complete their KWLs, SQ3Rs, and/or graphic organizers.

DEBRIEFING

5. Discuss the passage and the materials that they have completed.
6. Have students write summaries of their KWLs, SQ3Rs, and/or graphic organizers.

LEARNING LOGS

■ *Learning logs* are another type of journal that captures prereading, while-reading, and after-reading experiences and reflections so that students have the chance to reflect on all of the processes that they have engaged to understand the text (Commander & Smith, 1996). This helps them see changes in their thinking and growth in their development as they grow as readers and writers.

Learning logs can also be used narrowly. Short focus questions can be used to prompt students to write about books they are reading for class or selecting on their own for independent reading. For example, students might be asked to list the characters found in stories that they are reading and offer characteristics about them. The teacher can gauge how deeply the students are thinking about what they are reading based on these entries.

Learning logs are also especially helpful for teaching students to write in the content areas. Math might not appear to lend itself immediately to writing, beyond word problems, but there are aspects that can be easily included as reading log entries. For example, there are a number of declarative and procedural aspects to math that can be captured in print. Declarative knowledge is factual knowledge about addition, subtraction, multiplication, and division. Procedural knowledge is understanding the order of procedures necessary to solve a problem. Consider the following:

$$5 + 5X(6 + 3) = 50$$

This equation can become part of an important entry into a learning log:

1. The first thing I have to do is add the 6 and the 3 together because I have to do the things in the parentheses first.
2. The formula looks like this now: $5 + 5X(9) = 50$. I have to do the multiplication next and take 5X times 9. This gives me 45X.
3. The formula looks like this now: $5 + 45X = 40$. I have to get 45X alone, so I subtract 5 from both sides.

4. The formula looks like this now: $45X = 45$. I divide each side by 45 to get X alone and I get…

5. 1!!! X equals one!!

The math example shows the student's thought processes for each step in the problem. Understandings and misunderstandings that may have gone unnoticed or unvoiced are clarified through this process.

To this point, the text has covered both the learning-to-read and reading-to-learn processes. Next are other areas of support, including oral and written language development.

LEVEL 5: ORAL AND WRITTEN LANGUAGE DEVELOPMENT

This level of the model is about using oral and written language activities to develop the children's ability to read and understand narrative and expository text through speaking and writing activities.

Oral language activities are presented below that involve whole- and small-group discussions about literature since they transfer easily to the test. These activities are divided into two groups. Some discussions are meant to solidify the metacognitive strategies that students apply to texts when reading, while others are for discussions about literary elements.

Some written language activities were examined during the discussion about reading logs and dialectical journals. While these activities can certainly be part of this area, the specific activities here fall along a continuum. The written-language activities target emergent, developing, and proficient readers and writers. These activities are the language experience approach, paragraph response frames, and broader research-writing activities. See Table 2.18.

Oral Language Development

Oral language activities that promote literacy development are divided into strategy-based and literacy-based activities (Fielding & Pearson, 1994). Strategic discussions are first.

Strategy discussions provide students with opportunities to identify and practice the strategies that we discussed earlier in while-reading strategies for comprehension, like a think aloud (Anderson & Roit, 1993). They assume that students are already aware of strategies such as self-questioning and have some prior experience applying them to narrative and expository text. The goal is to provide students with practice in identifying what they can and should do when they encounter text that they do not immediately understand (Klinger & Vaughn, 1999).

TABLE 2.18   Oral and Written Language Development

ORAL LANGUAGE ACTIVITIES		WRITTEN LANGUAGE ACTIVITIES		
Strategy Discussions	Literacy Discussions	Emergent	Developing	Proficient
Strategy building	Structured discussions Literature circles	LEA	Story frames	Writing process

The general procedures for these types of discussions are as follows (Gagne, 1985; Johnson & Johnson, 1984; Kagan, 1984; McKenzie, 1979).

TEACHER PREPARATION

1. Select a variety of passages from a number of print sources such as books, magazines, and newspapers that can be dissected using strategic reading strategies.
2. Set the purpose for the activity from the beginning, so that the students understand what they are about to engage: "We're going to learn how to apply the strategies that we have been using in class to understand difficult parts of stories."

TEACHER MODELING

3. Activate prior knowledge about the strategies. Have the students write on strategies that they have used and then collect these strategies on the board (for example, think-alouds, structural analysis, etc.)

GUIDED PRACTICE

4. Read the passage with the students and pause at predetermined selections.
5. Ask the students to select a strategy from all of the ones that are available.
6. Apply the strategy together.

INDEPENDENT PRACTICE

7. Provide opportunities to apply a variety of reading strategies independently on grade-level texts.

Directed Reading and Reciprocal Activities.   Directed reading and reciprocal activities also help students to learn how to make predictions prior to reading and to confirm or negate them while reading to improve comprehension (Bear & McIntosh, 1990; Rosenshine & Meister, 1994). Strategies are a part of these activities; however, the focus is mainly on reading texts for specific purposes that may include predicting and confirming ideas or distinguishing fact from opinion. The idea is to use collaboration to provide students with some autonomy in the reading-to-learn process.

The steps for an activity that analyzes facts and opinions in a text are as follows (Alvermann & Hayes, 1989; Armbruster, Anderson, & Ostertag, 1987; Fitzgerald & Spiegel, 1983; Pearson & Dole, 1987).

TEACHER MODELING

1. Have students read the title and headings and make predictions about
   - what the passage will be about.
   - which ideas from the headings will need factual support.
   - what positions will be taken on each of the ideas drawn from the headings.

GUIDED PRACTICE

2. Read the article using the list of items generated in the first step.
3. Discuss which predictions have factual support and which do not.

INDEPENDENT PRACTICE

4. Close the activity by having the students separate the ideas that are fact from the ideas that are only opinions.

Literature Discussions.   Literature discussions are broad types of oral language activities that do not focus exclusively on strategies or specific purposes for reading. Instead, these activities ask students to analyze and understand texts in terms of higher-level thinking. Structured discussions and literature circles are two examples of these activities.

Literature discussions teach students two important things: first, how to discuss literature in deeper ways; second, how to conduct such discussions appropriately (Johnson & Johnson, 1989/1990). Learning how to work in a literature group can be just as important as learning how to discuss a particular reading (Johnson & Johnson, 1989/1990). Structured discussions can accomplish both goals. As students discuss higher-order questions about literature or expository text, the teacher awards points for the behaviors that the teacher wants the students to emulate and takes away points for behaviors that detract from the process, like being disruptive, aggressive, or making few meaningful contributions.

Literature discussions also ask students to discuss books that they have been reading in class or independently. The focus of the discussion may vary each week, from what they have been reading about to specific features of literature that they have explored in classroom reading (for example, metaphor, symbol, foreshadowing). For example, data charts can be configured to include setting, symbol, and metaphor and used during the literature discussion (McKenzie, 1979). The results of these small-group discussions can be captured on a chart and presented to the whole class. Table 2.19 shows an example of such a data chart.

As the students discuss each aspect of the setting, the symbols, and the metaphors in the text, their comments are listed in the chart. Presentations follow the discussions, so that the whole class can see how these story elements are found in a variety of works that the children have been reading.

Written Language Development

For the test, you also need to understand the role that written language activities play in this model. The purpose and name of the activities that you need to know for the test are these:

Emergent	Language experience approaches
Developing	Story frames
Proficient	Writing process

As you can see, the activities in this section help students learn the writing process from the emergent to the proficient stages. Emergent activities are described first.

TABLE 2.19   Data Chart

	SETTING	SYMBOLS	METAPHORS
Chris			
Mary			

Language Experience Approach. The language experience approach (LEA) that is described in the section on concepts about print is an effective method for teaching students early writing skills. Students learn how to write single sentences about experiences that they have had recently or are going to have in the class or on a field trip. These sentences can be as simple as early pre-phonetic scribbling to later stages of phonetic and transitional spelling.

The major principle is to teach children that what they say can be written down and read to teach them the symbolic nature of language (Shanahan, 1988). The sentences can be collected in a notebook and these sentences can be the first things that the children read independently. LEA activities also help teachers keep alphabetical lists of a child's known words. These known words can be used during reading to prompt the students when they get stuck or as words for phonics instruction.

Following are the characteristics of LEAs that you should know.

1. Very early LEA instruction has the teacher writing down sentences exactly as the student says them, regardless of grammar. The student dictates a sentence to the teacher. For example, an utterance like "I goed to buy presents yesterday" would be written down word for word. The teacher and student practice reading the student's utterance together. Changes to the grammar, such as changing *goed* to *went,* can take place later on as the child encounters these structures in separate instruction.
2. Later, the student attempts to write the stories that they have recited orally. The teacher may have to write a "child-to-English" translation below the sentence, as in Figure 2.15.
3. As the student grows more proficient, the teacher asks the child to spell sight words correctly and to use letter boxes as part of the activity, as discussed in the section of this chapter on spelling instruction.

Story Frames. As students become more and more proficient in writing single words, sentences, and lengthier writings, structure developmental writing activities are used. The most common tool used for this purpose is the paragraph frame (Lewis, Wray, & Rospigliosi, 1994). Story frames provide a scaffold to transition students from simple ideas about writing words and sentences to writing full paragraphs. The frames provide an outline that the teacher creates and the students complete. Following is an example.

The title of the story is _____. It is about _____.
There are _____ characters in the story. Their names are _____.

The structure of the paragraph frame can be expanded to include answers to literal and inferential comprehension questions (*who, what, where, why,* and *how*). This facilitates the

I like my dog

FIGURE 2.15 "Child-to-English" Translation

early development of the writing process, along with learning how to answer comprehension questions (Fowler, 1982).

Writing Process.   Activities for proficient writers teach students the writing process. These activities also help students think about how formats and language work together. The format of a personal letter, for example, is different from the format of a business letter that refuses a customer's request. But the largest activity is the process approach that moves the child's writing from its earliest inception to its final product.

The writing process follows five steps (Hoffman, 1998). You should know them for the test.

1. Prewriting	Brainstorming ideas for a topic
	Generating an outline
2. Drafting	Writing each section of the outline
	Finding support for ideas within the outline
3. Revising	Organizing ideas
	Peer-reviewing drafts
	Elaborating content
4. Editing	Editing for style
	Fixing grammar and spelling
5. Publishing	Developing classroom collections

The artifacts that are collected in portfolios come directly from each phase of the writing process. Each area of the writing process is explained in the list that follows.

1. Prewriting activities help students to brainstorm topics for writing. This can be done by having the students free-write ideas on a topic or list what they know and what they have learned about a subject. These ideas can be organized into an outline or graphic organizer that is used as the basis for the writing phase of the process.
2. Drafting activities ask students to use their outlines as a framework for writing. Here, students begin to fill out each part of the outline with sentences and seek sources (for example, citations and quotations) that support their ideas.
3. During the revising phase, students share their outlines and their writing with peers or with the teacher during writing conferences. By receiving feedback on the topic, the supporting ideas, and the writing, students have the opportunity to make changes to their writing before they polish it on its way to a publishable form.
4. Editing occurs when the students review the final work for style and grammar. Working either independently or with peers, students look at the types of sentences that they have selected and try to verify their order and length, along with fixing basic grammar and spelling errors that appear in the piece.
5. Publishing the students' work can take the form of classroom anthologies, newspapers, magazines, to name a few examples. Here, all of the students' polished pieces are collected for the students to read.

Students learn that writing is a process and that essays do not appear magically; instead, they must be cultivated and developed over time.

Instructing Grammar Points. The research process includes polishing and publishing phases in which students find and fix problems with organization, style, and grammar. Explicit instruction in each of these areas must occur first if the students are to be expected to fix structural, stylistic, or grammatical problems.

On the test, you may be asked questions about how to teach each one of these elements or to identify problems with them in student data. The following is a basic discussion of organization, style, and grammar that will be helpful for such questions.

Organization	Introduction
	Thesis
	Body paragraphs
	Conclusion
Style	Parallelism
	Redundancy
	Passives
	Transitions
Grammar	Subject/verb agreement
	Comma splices
	Run-on sentences
	Sentence fragments

Organization. When reviewing student essay data, look for organizational patterns in the essay and within each paragraph. What you are looking for is the basic five-paragraph essay that uses an introduction, thesis, body paragraphs, and conclusion. Within each paragraph, you are looking for topic sentences, sequenced supporting details, and a concluding sentence. Table 2.20 shows a generic five-part essay on spelling development.

When you review student data on the test, look for the five essay components and at the structure of the body paragraphs, since they may reveal needs that you have to identify in multiple-choice or short-answer questions (Essay outlines or paragraph frames are appropriate for developing organizational skills.)

Style. You may also be asked to review student writing for style. The items below reflect examples of the major stylistic considerations that you should know for the test.

Parallelism	Incorrect: Swimming and to run are my favorite activities.
	Correct: Swimming and running are my favorite activities.
Redundancy	Incorrect: Students need to write. Students need to study. Students need to learn.
	Correct: Students need to write, study, and learn.
Passives	Incorrect: The book was read by the boy.
	Correct: The boy read the book.

If the organizational pattern of the sample data looks acceptable and the paragraphs are sequenced properly, then you may have to look at the style. Problems with parallelism are easy to identify: In the example from the list above, the writer has not used the same

TABLE 2.20   Five-Paragraph Essay

Introduction/thesis	There are three stages in spelling development. The stages are pre-phonetic, phonetic, and transitional. Each one has different characteristics and activities.
Body paragraph	Pre-phonetic spelling is the first and earliest stage of spelling. It is characterized by scribbling lines or using symbols arbitrarily to represent letters. Letter-sound activities help students move to the second phase of spelling development.
Body paragraph	Phonetic spelling is the second stage of spelling development. A child's spelling of the dominant sounds heard at the beginnings and endings of words typify this stage. Learning to encode medial sounds through letter-box activities are common at this developmental level.
Body paragraph	Transitional spelling is a later stage of spelling development. Here, the child encodes all of the major sounds heard in the word, but may need additional work in spelling patterns. This helps the child move into the conventional stage of spelling.
Conclusion	The pre-phonetic, phonetic, and transitional stages are part of spelling development, and each one has its own characteristics and required activities.

form of the words that are in the subject. Redundancies are also easy to spot since the data may show a student who is repeating the same words or phrases throughout the paragraph. Passive voice sentences are pretty simple to find, too. Look for the characteristic "was + verb" and a *by*-phrase: "The dog was walked by his owner."

Grammar. Space does not permit a full review of English grammar. However, there are common grammar errors that you can spot in data sets.

Subject-verb agreement	Incorrect: He walk to his house yesterday. Correct: He walked to his house yesterday.
Comma splices	Incorrect: He walked to his house yesterday, he had dinner with his family. Correct: He walked to his house yesterday, and he had dinner with his family.
Run-ons	Incorrect: He walked to his house yesterday he had dinner with his family. Correct: He walked to his house yesterday. He had dinner with his family.
Fragments	Incorrect: When he walked home yesterday. He had dinner with his family. Correct: When he walked home yesterday, he had dinner with his family.

Look at the verbs in the data. If they do not agree with the subject in number or tense, they show areas of need. Comma splices, too, might be present. A comma splice occurs when a student "staples" two complete sentences together with a comma instead of using a period to end one sentence before beginning another or joining them together with a conjunction. Run-on sentences are similar to comma splices, only lazier. Here, the writer not only leaves off a conjunction, but also forgets to supply a comma. Sentence fragments are usually sentences that begin with what's called a subordinating conjunction. You'll know them when you read them because the thought seems incomplete without the addition of a complete sentence.

You might be asked to identify activities that help students to improve their use of English syntax. Sentence strips and cloze activities are likely candidates for such questions.

Sentence Strips. Sentence strips (Clay, 1993b) are an activity that help children learn proper syntax. They use either the child's actual writing or sentences that feature particular grammar points that the teacher wants to instruct. Following is an example using a sentence that the child has written. Here, the child has written a sentence in the passive voice and the teacher wants to show the child how to phrase it in the active voice (adapted from Clay, 1993b).

1. Write the child's sentence down on a strip of paper and ask him to cut the sentence into individual words.
2. Have the child put the cards in the order in which the sentence was written.

3. Teach the rule for creating active sentences, where the actor is placed in first position and the receiver of the action is placed after the verb.
4. Show the child how to move the cards into the active voice.

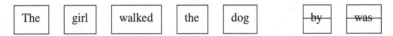

5. Have the child locate other sentences in his writing that are in the passive voice and use the same activity on them.

Cloze Activities. Cloze activities are also used to teach grammar points (Barnitz, 1998). The term *cloze* is a fancy term for *fill in the blank.* These activities ask children to rely on syntactic and semantic cues to place the correct words in spaces. This can be adapted to teaching grammar points such as article placement. Following is an example.

TEACHER PREPARATION
1. Develop a paragraph that omits articles before certain nouns.

_____ apple hung from _____ tree. _____ worm crawled up _____ branch.

TEACHER MODELING
2. Teach the students that the article *a* is used before words that begin with consonants and that *an* is used before words that begin with vowels.

GUIDED PRACTICE
3. Ask the students to work together to supply the correct article in each of the spaces.
4. Review the passage with the students for accuracy.

INDEPENDENT PRACTICE
5. Apply the rule in reading and have the students locate other words that take the articles *a* and *an.*

The same activity can be adapted to any number of grammar points (for example, inflectional endings, adverb endings, subject-verb agreement).

The next section moves from individual activities to something much larger: classroom and unit planning. All of the areas of the model influence both of these areas.

LEVEL 6: CLASSROOM AND UNIT PLANNING

In this section, the following topics about classroom and unit planning are discussed.

Classroom organization	Selecting texts
	Arranging centers
	Grouping students
Unit planning	Thematic units
	Interdisciplinary units

The model that you have just learned about affects your considerations in each of these areas. The learning-to-read and reading-to-learn distinction is one to keep in mind as you consider the areas of classroom and unit planning discussed next. For example, the texts, centers, groups, and units for children who are learning to read support early decoding and fluency, while the same areas for children who are reading to learn are aimed at developing vocabulary and comprehension. You can imagine that as the students move upward in the model, so do the activities that the children engage in.

Classroom Organization

Following are areas of classroom organization that you should know for the test, including guidelines for selecting texts, creating centers, grouping students, and planning thematic and interdisciplinary units.

Selecting Texts.   It is important for you to know about the basis for selecting and using literature in the classroom. Three areas are covered in this section: the types of texts available for consideration, the features of these available texts, and their role in literacy instruction. Each of these areas is discussed separately.

There are four types of text that you should know about for the exam: wordless books, decodable books, predictable books, and authentic literature. Ideally, a teacher selects among these types of books to instruct students in reading, depending on the needs of the students in the classroom. The grade-level expectations and the types of activities also influence the types of books that the teacher selects. As discussed earlier, the results of formal and informal assessments play a role in the types of texts used in the classroom. The results of emergent literacy assessments in kindergarten and first-grade classrooms tell you the kind of books that would benefit the students the most. Some classes need more wordless books in the beginning, while others require an abundance of decodable texts.

You may also have to demonstrate your knowledge of selecting texts based on classroom data or profiles. To answer these types of questions successfully, you need to understand the features and purposes of each of these four major types of texts. The items that follow relate the features and purposes of each type of text.

Wordless Books.   As their name implies, wordless books contain pictures of people, things, and actions that tell a story without print (Miller, 1998). For example, if you recall the nursery rhyme about the cow that jumped over the moon, you can easily imagine how such a story can be conveyed without words. The first page might show a cow and the moon together. The second page shows the cow running toward the moon. The third page captures the cow in midflight, and so on. The purpose of these types of texts is to help students who are not yet reading develop a number of important skills that they will come to rely on later in their development. These skills include oral language development, story grammar (for example, setting, plot, character), and basic comprehension skills (for example, who the characters are). Teachers and students "read" these books together to develop these capacities. Data reflecting children with no ability to decode print or with upper-elementary English language learners are also good candidates for these texts since they need to develop their spoken vocabularies.

Decodable Books.   Decodable text is the type of literature that this model favors for early literacy instruction. It uses phonetically regular patterns that correspond tightly to the rules and patterns that the students are learning through separate and isolated phonics instruction (Mesmer, 2001).

Decodable text serves three purposes: to support automatic word decoding skills, to provide opportunities to apply decoding skills in the context of reading, and to emphasize reliance on letter-sound decoding. This type of text provides students with the means with which to develop the fluent decoding of text that is the ultimate aim of phonics instruction.

An important feature of decodable text is its one-to-one correspondence with decoding skills instruction. If you recall that the components of phonics instruction begin with letter-sound correspondence, and move to simple onsets and rimes, complex letter combinations, and phonics generalizations, you will understand that decodable texts follow the same pattern. High-frequency sight words are also an important part of decodable text, so that the sight words that are taught in isolation are immediately found in the decodable text passages.

Here are some examples. Letter books like *A Is for Ape* teach the child the long and short sounds associated with the letter *a*. Decodable books might also focus on common letter patterns such as *-at: A cat sat on a mat.* The point is that decodable texts serve an important purpose in the classroom since they parallel the early-reading instruction that children receive. As the complexity of the phonics skills that are taught in isolation increases, so do the complexity patterns found in the decodable texts. The ideal situation is to have any skills taught in isolation be immediately reinforced in the text of the decodable book. Doing so will be an extension of the phonics skills that the child is acquiring in direct instruction.

Predictable Texts.   Predictable texts use the same pattern recursively to teach children to recognize common syntax and sight words (Park, 1982). The patterns use simple grammatical patterns and "kernel" sentences. The grammatical patterns can be subject-verb-object constructions, such as *The boy walked the dog.* The kernel sentences are declarative, interrogative, exclamatory, and conditional.

Declarative:	The boy walked the dog.
Interrogative:	Did the boy walk the dog?
Exclamatory:	Walk the dog!
Conditional:	If the boy walks the dog, then the dog walks the boy.

Pictures usually accompany the print to add greater context to the sentences. They are "sing-songy" and use catchy phrasing to engage children in the reading. They can become favorites of children because they are easy to manage and the refrains are often "catchy."

This model tends to favor decodable text over predictable text for the following reasons.

1. Students may rely exclusively on the pattern and not on the print. Once they recognize the pattern, they may simply apply it to every page, giving the illusion of reading. Decodable text is linked directly to the skills that the teacher is teaching, so the children must rely on the print when reading decodable books. This may not be the case with predictable books.

2. Reading by pattern is a strategy that might work for predictable texts but will not work for decodable or authentic texts, where the language and patterns are not controlled as tightly. Students learn to decode words by letter patterns and not through refrains. According to this model, letter-pattern decoding leads to automatic decoding more quickly and transfers more easily to authentic text.

3. The pictures may interfere with decoding. As stated earlier during the discussion of fluency, attention is an important consideration in this model. If the students' attention is occupied by making mistakes, correcting errors, attempting to comprehend, or looking at pictures above the text, he might not learn to decode properly. This model is very strict when it comes to attaining fluency; nothing can stand in the way of its acquisition.

The next section presents authentic texts and how they should be incorporated into the classroom.

Authentic Literature.   Authentic literature is the final type of material that you need to know for the test. Literature of this kind is not altered to suit decodable letter patterns, nor are the sentences altered for predictability. Instead, they are written with topics in mind that appeal to the age or maturity level of the children. The language used in the texts may be simplified, and the authors may use words that are likely to be familiar ones to the student or at least in the students' speaking or listening vocabularies. Furthermore, high numbers of polysyllabic words might be left out of authentic texts in the early grades. Authentic literature is closer to real-world writing than are decodable or predictable texts, since it is not as contrived and controlled as the other types of literature are.

You should know something about selecting authentic texts for your classroom. There are three important areas in this general process.

1. The students' cultures should be represented in the books and magazines that you select for this purpose. You should also select multicultural texts that offer realistic, nonstereotypical representations of multicultural families, historical figures, and stories (Yokota, 1993). Cultural folktales, stories, and traditions are also important additions to the collection (Bieger, 1995/1996).
2. The students' interests should be represented well. Student reading interest surveys might include questions about what they want to read. Based on that information, the teacher can select books, magazines, or other media to ensure that the children can find what they are looking for.
3. All of the students should be able to locate materials that are written at their independent reading levels. The idea is to try to locate multicultural literature and high-interest materials that are accessible to all of the students in the class. This means that you have to know the independent reading levels of all of the students, along with their cultures and interest.

The model also values including a wide variety of genres of authentic texts, including narratives, expository texts, journals, magazines, children's newspapers, and so on. This way, the children have more exposure to print in a variety of media that is accessible to them, regardless of their reading levels.

Arranging Centers. Knowing how to develop and monitor literacy centers is another potential target of the exam. Centers are areas of the classroom in which small groups of students work together or individual students work privately. Centers can also be places in which the teacher groups students with similar needs together for minilessons.

The centers are sensitive to the levels of development discussed in the model. During the learning-to-read phase, the centers are mainly for learning the components of decoding, automacity, and fluency. During reading to learn, students may also use centers for the writing process. The centers include brainstorming, drafting, revising, editing, and publishing stations for the students to use for each phase of the writing process.

In addition to student levels, the four skills of reading, writing, listening, and speaking are a part of planning literacy centers. Centers can be designed around these areas in the following ways.

1. The reading center should be near the classroom library where books can be easily selected and brought to a quiet, comfortable, well-lit part of the room. The area can be distinguished in a special way so that it is an appealing place for the children to take their books to be read quietly.
2. The writing center should have all of the materials needed for writing: paper, pens, pencils, and so on. Theme centers are another possibility, where the writing center becomes a post office with stationery, stamps, and envelopes. The children can write letters to characters in stories or to classmates using authentic materials for this purpose.

3. Listening centers can include prerecorded books that the teacher has created, so that the students can listen to tapes as they follow along in their books. The purpose is to help students connect speech and print and to learn the proper intonation patterns that makes "book talk" sound like "real talk."

4. Speaking centers can be used for playing phonics games, paired reading, or project work. The idea is to create a literacy center where discussion and activity are permitted. This center is located in a part of the room that offers the least amount of distraction to the other centers being used.

Teachers can monitor centers through anecdotal observation and student comments. If the children seem to be off task most of the time or if there is no relationship between the time spent at the centers and assessments, adjustments in the activities might be in order. Also, soliciting student comments gives the teacher an indication of what the students find most useful about the center and what needs to be changed.

Grouping Students. There are two types of student groups that you need to know about for the test. These include homogeneous groupings and heterogeneous groupings. Each type of arrangement serves a different purpose.

Homogeneous Groups. Homogeneous groupings are ability groups in which students who share the same need in skills or strategies are taught together in minilessons. These arrangements are valued on the test. For example, if the results of a phonics assessment show that five students have trouble with blends in the initial positions of words, five other students have difficulty decoding digraphs in the final positions of words, and five more cannot read diphthongs, the students are grouped around their common need.

After grouping the students by need, the teacher develops lessons for blends, digraphs, and diphthongs. Explicit instruction takes place, in which the teacher directly teaches the skill, provides guided practice for the students, and then asks them to apply the skill independently. This model of instruction is appropriate for all areas of the model, including concepts about print, phonemic awareness, phonics, spelling, fluency, vocabulary, and comprehension. Peer-to-peer teaching is not favored in this model, by the way. This method of instruction is viewed as placing the burden of instruction on the shoulders of students who are not qualified to provide this level of instruction. Do not select answers that place students in the role of teacher.

Guided reading groups are another form of ability group. These groups are used to teach all of the aspects of decoding print, fluent reading, comprehending vocabulary, and using strategies to understand narrative and expository text before, during, and after reading (Manzo, 1975). The teacher uses multiple copies of the same instructional-level texts that the students have, and the group works to learn skills and strategies together. For example, the teacher might begin with a concept about print activity, in which she asks the students to locate the title and point to where to start reading. She might then ask the students to decode the title using initial letter and letter-pattern strategies in the process. Then, the students might offer predictions of what the story is about and the group reads together to confirm or negate these predictions.

While the students read the text, the teacher can choral-read portions of it to help the students develop a sensitivity to intonation and fluency. Choral reading is used throughout the activities to avoid embarrassing students unnecessarily, as reading aloud by one's self in a small group might. She can also use think alouds as the group reads together to teach the students to apply sequencing questions to the story or to predict what might happen next. Difficult vocabulary words are syllabicated and analyzed structurally so that the students can learn how to apply such strategies in the context of reading. Finally, the group can use elaboration activities to create stories together about what they have read.

In sum, guided reading groups offer skill-and-strategy instruction for homogenous groups of students who share common needs and reading levels. All areas of the model can be used in these arrangements.

Heterogeneous Groups. Heterogeneous groupings, in which students of varying levels and talents work together to apply strategies that they have learned in prior instruction, are permitted for certain activities in this model. They are appropriate for all of the brainstorming activities discussed for vocabulary development and reading comprehension, such as semantic mapping and predicting what stories might be about (Johnson & Johnson, 1984; Kagan, 1986). In addition, heterogeneous groups are also allowed for instances when students are applying strategies that they have learned in separate instruction. For example, the strategy discussion activity that you learned about during oral language activities can be grouped heterogeneously, provided that all of the members can select among known strategies. Heterogeneous groups are also useful for providing English as a second language students opportunities to hear and use English in a social context, so long as peer-to-peer teaching is not the focus of the interaction (peer-to-peer practice is fine).

Unit Planning

Understanding how to develop units of instruction is also valuable for the test. There are two types of units that you should understand: the interdisciplinary unit and the thematic unit. The distinctions are slight. Interdisciplinary units join together two or more content areas, such as math and language arts. The content areas are the focus of interdisciplinary units, as seen in the example of using a learning log to explain the processes that one might use to solve equations. In that example, language arts is used to support the study of a math concept. Of course, since it is a unit, the depth of the exploration is much deeper than just writing out procedures for math problems, but this example suffices as a direct example.

Thematic units are different to a degree from interdisciplinary units (Meyers, 1993). Here, a theme such as "change over time" might be explored using a multidisciplinary approach, rather then emphasizing how one content area can be combined with another to support learning. For example, the teacher might select literature in which the characters make meaningful changes by growing up or growing old. The same theme might be applied to biology, where tadpoles are observed over time as they become frogs or larvae become butterflies. Math can also be used in calculating the number of times that a ball bounces when dropped from a particular height. The point is to look at some broad theme or idea from a variety of angles and content areas.

To help you to understand the kinds of units that the model values, here are guidelines for an interdisciplinary unit (adapted from Shanahan, 1997).

1. Select topics that can be explored through different disciplines (for example, the growth cycle).
2. Define clear phases for the activity. The first phase might emphasize one content area before another. For example, the students might "do the science" for the growth cycle first, and then use language arts activities on the same topic or theme in the second phase of the activity.
3. Select activities that the students use to explore the topic in a deep way. For example, a science experiment would be an appropriate way to explore the growth cycle in phase one, and a research-based language arts activity that utilizes each phase of the writing process in the second phase would be appropriate.
4. Set the time for each phase and balance the activities throughout the unit.

Following is an example unit that exemplifies each of these principles.

1. Science and language arts can be used in an interdisciplinary on the growth cycle for upper-elementary students.
2. During the first phase of the unit, emphasize exploring the growth cycle through a science experiment. First, develop small, manageable groups of students who would receive different kinds of seeds, soil, water, and fertilizer for the experiment. They would plant the seeds in different ways and create three different conditions for them. Some seeds would be planted in one container and receive only water for nourishment. The seeds in another contain would receive water and fertilizer. The seeds in the last container would receive water, fertilizer, and sunlight. Each group of students would care for each plant over a three-week period and measure growth on charts, draw illustrations of the changes, and note characteristics in their learning logs.
3. As the plants change, students would also develop research projects on which plants will grow best and why they believe that this is so. These hypotheses would be used as the basis for a written report that would use the writing process. Working in small groups, students would research the growth cycle and the roles of soil, water, fertilizer, and sunlight in plant growth through classroom resources, the library, and the Internet. They would write up what they have learned about each topic, along with whether their early hypotheses about which plants would produce the most growth and why were correct. They would apply editing for organization and polishing for style and grammar to their writing in preparation for the publishing phase of their reports.
4. The final product for the unit would incorporate each group's research on the growth cycle and the role of each of the factors in the growth of the plants. Students would use the growth charts that they had kept, the drawings that they had made, and the written descriptions that they had noted to create visual displays of their findings, which could then be presented to the class. They could also create a classroom science journal that would incorporate the students' findings on the growth cycle and how different conditions affect the growth of plants.

In sum, thematic and interdisciplinary units explore themes through the content areas. The ideal units in this model are those that incorporate broad activities that rely on a variety of skills for the purpose of exploration, reading, writing, and communicating. Be sure to consider the reading-to-learn and learning-to-read distinction: Themes for younger children are simplified and familiar, while they are more complex for upper-elementary children. It is also helpful for you to review other interdisciplinary units prior to the exam. *Instructor* magazine is available at most universities, and it includes a new unit plan each month. Many of these are thematic and interdisciplinary. Take the time to review several of these units, as they may be very handy for the exam.

CONCLUSION

You have learned all about the model described in Chapter 1. You have seen how assessment of individuals and groups of students is conducted, along with all of the components of the learning-to-read and reading-to-learn processes and their assessments and activities. You have also learned about how classroom and unit planning are affected by different areas of the model. Additional information about the content that you need to know for the exam is posted at http://www.ablongman.com/boosalis as it becomes available.

The next chapters discuss how to complete the written portions of the exam (Chapter 3) and the multiple-choice portions (Chapter 4). It is important for you to read both chapters, regardless of whether your exam has essays. Chapter 5 helps you apply the methods from Chapters 3 and 4. Chapter 6's study plan requires you to answer essay questions that will help you whether you face written responses or not. In short, you cannot simply read the contents of Chapter 2 and expect to be prepared; instead, you must actively study the information. Chapter 6 helps you do just that.

CHAPTER THREE

MAGIC ESSAYS

This chapter primarily covers the essay portions of the exams, but it also includes valuable information for candidates who face multiple-choice-only exams. While it is specifically designed to help you if you must write essays on the exam, do not skip this chapter if your test has no essays. The first reason is that you need to learn data analysis methods, and this chapter covers those methods for you. Furthermore, many of the multiple-choice questions are structured just like these essays and require answers that follow the forms described in this chapter. Understanding these formats and their functions will help you to pick out correct answers on the test. In short, whether your test has essays or not, this chapter is an important one for you to read and understand.

HOW WAS THE CONTENT OF CHAPTER 3 DEVELOPED?

Boosalis (2003) establishes the major formats and question types used on reading-instruction exams. Through an exhaustive review of the bulletins and all of the available data sets to generate the forms. There are four major types of essays that you must learn to write: justifications, lessons plans for decoding or comprehension, instructional procedures, and case studies. We generated the sample questions based on these examples.

Other essay formats may be required for your exam. Be sure to obtain any available study guides. See your official registration bulletin for the order form. You may also visit http://www.ablongman.com/boosalis for links to your state's department of education, which may allow you to download the study guide. Restrictions may apply to who is allowed to order or download these materials, so read any printed or online disclaimers first before attempting to obtain the information.

EFFECTIVE WRITTEN-RESPONSE OUTLINES

You should memorize the essay forms in Table 3.1 for the written portion of the test. These formats allow you to write answers to the questions very quickly, and they also help you to understand the information in the rest of this chapter. If your test does not have a written portion, you need not memorize the information; however, familiarize yourself with the formats because many of the multiple-choice formats may ask you to select items that fall

TABLE 3.1 **Essay Formats**

JUSTIFICATION ESSAY (DOMAIN I)	NEEDS-BASED LESSON PLAN (DOMAIN II) DECODING	NEEDS-BASED LESSON PLAN (DOMAIN III) COMPREHENSION	PROCEDURAL ESSAY (DOMAIN IV)	CASE STUDY (DOMAIN I–IV)
¶ How	¶ Need	¶ Need	¶ What	¶ Strength 1
¶ Why	¶ Lesson plan	¶ Lesson plan	¶ How (steps)	¶ Strength 2
¶ Benefit	¶ Benefit	¶ Benefit	¶ Benefit	¶ Problem + Need A and B
				¶ Need A + minilesson plan + benefit
				¶ Need B + minilesson plan + benefit

Credit: California Reader, 2003, vol. 36, p. 26
Source: C. N. Boosalis, 2003, Effective time-management models for the constructed response portion of the Reading Instruction Competence Assessment, *The California Reader*, 36, 26–36.

under each category of justification, lesson plan, procedure, or case study. These outlines are applied to Chapter 2 through Chapter 6.

To help you to understand the purpose of each essay, let's look at the function of each one.

- Justification essays might ask you to state why an assessment or instructional activity "works," in which you state why an assessment or activity is used in the classroom, how the assessment or activity functions, and what benefit the assessment or activity brings to the learning situation.
- Needs-based lesson plans may require you to analyze data sets and then write a three-paragraph essay that identifies the need present in the data, a lesson plan for the identified need, and a statement of the benefit of the activity.
- Procedural essays may require you to describe assessment tools or activities that are appropriate for a given assessment or instructional situation.
- Case studies ask you to analyze a variety of data sets to write a complex essay. Because case studies tend to be the longest pieces of writing, they are addressed first.

WRITING THE CASE STUDY

Writing the case study is easy, once you know how to do it. Here is an example question.

This case study focuses on a student named Chris. The data sets below describe his reading performance during the early part of third grade. Using this data set, write a response in which you apply your knowledge of literacy development to this case. Your response should include three parts:

- Item 1: State three strengths and/or needs reflected in the data.
- Item 2: Write two lesson plans for this student.
- Item 3: Explain how these lesson plans will help the student's development.

As the three item statements show, you have three tasks in your writing. For Item 1, you have to identify strengths and needs. The strengths and needs are drawn from your analysis of the student data to be presented next. Item 2 requires you to write two lesson plans for this student. These lesson plans are based on your findings from your analyses of the student data. Finally, Item 3 asks you to state two benefits of the activities that you offer in Item 2. To receive full credit, you must not only identify all three elements correctly, but also organize the answers such that evaluators can find them quickly and unmistakably. Look at it this way. If the people who read your essay cannot find what they are looking for immediately, they are likely to give you a low score.

Before looking at how to write the case, look at the following basic data and the analyses that are required for them (Table 3.2). When analyzing a case, use the model described in Chapter 2. The specific areas that you should consider are from Levels 2 through 4.

Start with fluency at Level 3. If the data reflect problems with fluency, look back at the area of decoding. You will probably find that the data reflect problems in concepts about print, phonemic awareness, phonics, sight words, or automatic word decoding. However, if fluency is present, look at the child's comprehension. Ask yourself if the child's vocabulary skills are sufficient, if the child has literal and inferential comprehension, and so forth. Exploring the data with this model in mind helps you to view the data properly, in order to begin to develop your case study around the strengths and needs, instructional strategies, and benefits. Perform this activity regardless of whether the data are from grades K–3 or from 4–8, since learning to read can continue into the upper grades depending on whether fluency is present. You must be flexible in your analyses when interpreting grade-level data.

You may also see data in the form of anecdotal records (Rhodes & Nathenson-Mejia, 1993) that include teacher notes on a student's behavior during sustained silent reading, parent concerns during conferences, or the student's general progress on exams, content, activities, or assessments. These notes are a good place to find indications about strengths and needs, but do not use them as the sole basis for your observations. In this model, test data in the form of standardized assessments, informal reading inventories, and so forth are the best resources to use to support your contentions; anecdotal records, on the other hand, may bolster your case, but not make it (so to speak).

Using the model in Table 3.2, analyze the data and make notes about the student's strengths and needs reflected therein.

TABLE 3.2   Levels 2, 3, and 4

Level 2: Decoding (Kindergarten through Third Grade)

| ■ Concepts about print | ■ Phonemic awareness | ■ Phonics | ■ Sight words | ■ Automacity |

Level 3: Fluency

Level 4: Comprehension (Third Grade through Eighth Grade)

| ■ Vocabulary instruction | ■ Literal, inferential, and evaluative comprehension | ■ Pre-, while-, and post-reading strategies | ■ Schema strategies |

DATA SET FOR CASE STUDY

Super Bowl Sunday was a day that Bob had been waiting for. It took forever for the day to arrive, and Bob looked forward to watching his favorite team, the Bulldogs, play the most important game of the season.

For weeks, he had cheered his team on. With his mother's help, he even called a radio program to offer the team support. Now, finally, the day arrived. His family even told him that it was his day the night before.

"Bob," his mother called, "I need to talk to you." Bob approached his mother. "Your cousin Martin is coming," she said. "His mother is very sick and we need to look after him for a couple of days."

Bob was mortified but said nothing. He knew that Martin had a disability and that he would scream louder than even Bob could if he didn't get his way. He also knew that Martin couldn't help it. Martin's favorite program was *Star Trek,* and it was on at the worst possible time.

TEACHER/STUDENT DIALOGUE

Teacher: Tell me what you were reading about.

Chris: It's a story about a boy named Bob who's going to watch the Super Bowl.

Teacher: What else can you tell me?

Chris: The name of the team is the Bulldogs. Oh, and his cousin Martin is coming.

Teacher: What can you tell me about Martin?

Chris: He likes *Star Trek.*

Teacher: Is there anything special about Martin?

Chris: Yes. He can scream louder than Bob can.

Teacher: How does Bob feel about Martin coming over?

Chris: Happy, because they get to watch the game together.

WRITING SUMMARY

This is a story about Bob. Bob likes football. He is going to watch the Super Bowl with his cousin, Martin. Martin is coming over because his mother is very sick. They are going to watch the game and have fun, because Martin can scream louder than Bob can.

You have four sets of data to consider for the case. The easiest items to look at are the student's test scores, shown in Table 3.3, because they reveal a definite trend for where the student's strengths and needs are. Starting with fluency, the test scores show that the student decodes text at grade level. This suggests that he should have enough attention left

TABLE 3.3

ASSESSMENT AREA	CHRIS'S SCORES	GOAL
1. Decoding	Third Grade	Third Grade
2. Spelling	6	5
3. Main ideas	4	5
4. Inferences	1	4
5. Polysyllabic words	3	5
6. Prefix/root/suffixes	1	5

over for comprehension. Also, the test scores, the teacher and student dialogue, and the student's writing sample demonstrate that this student has literal comprehension. However, there appears to be a lack of inferential comprehension. You can see this because the student did not grasp the fact that the character in the story is on the verge of anger because his cousin is coming over. Plus, the student's test scores show that vocabulary and making inferences may be areas that would help him to improve his inferential comprehension.

Data Analysis for the Case Study

This basic analysis tells you that the student has particular strengths and a major need. The next step is to begin to formulate your essay around the strengths and needs that you have identified. Remember that you have three tasks in this question:

- Item 1: State three strengths and/or needs reflected in the data
- Item 2: Write two lesson plans for this student
- Item 3: Explain how these lesson plans will help the student's development

Memorizing the schematic in Figure 3.1 will help you with this task. You should receive scratch paper to use for this purpose during the test.

The numbered items show the items that you will put in each of the paragraphs. Numbers one and two identify the strengths in the student's data (decoding and literal comprehension), number three is the paragraph that states the major problem (inferential comprehension of narrative text), and numbers four and five contain the lesson plans for the areas that need attention to help the student develop inferential comprehension (vocabulary development and making inferences).

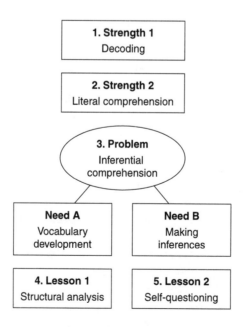

FIGURE 3.1

TABLE 3.4 Example Answer to the Case Study Question

FORM	CONTENT
■ 1	
Strength 1	The student's test data show that he can decode at grade level. This means that he reads with adequate fluency and accuracy and that he should have enough attention available to try to comprehend what he is reading.
■ 2	
Strength 2	The teacher/student dialogue, his writing sample, and his test scores show that he does comprehend what he read literally. For example, he is able to identify factual information from the teacher's oral questions, and he can even summarize these ideas in writing.
■ 3	
Problem	However, the student has a major problem with inferential comprehension, since he could not infer the problem that the main character is having with the fact that his cousin is coming over
Need A	during the Super Bowl. This may be because he has no strategies available to him to
Need B	comprehend higher-level vocabulary words such as "mortified." Also, he may not have any strategies that will help him to make inferences as he reads text.
■ 4	
Need A	To help the student comprehend higher-level vocabulary words, the teacher should combine
Lesson plan	structural analysis with contextual analysis. First, she should build on his syllabication strengths and teach him how to analyze the syllables for prefixes, suffixes, and roots. Then, the student should practice this strategy on selected words to ensure that he can do it. Next, the teacher should show the student how to reassemble the word and check the context of the sentence to confirm the
Benefit	meaning of the word. These activities would help the student to comprehend unfamiliar vocabulary words and would greatly increase his chances to comprehend text inferentially.
■ 5	
Need B	The student also needs to learn how to use self-questioning to make inferences while he reads.
Lesson plan	The teacher should use the passage and model how to ask questions during the reading. For example, she could model how to ask, "What is Martin like? Is Bob really happy about his coming over? Why does the last sentence say that this is the worst possible time for Martin
Benefit	to come to stay?" Learning how to ask and answer these questions will help the student to make inferences as he is reading the text.

Writing the Case Study

Now you are in a position to write the essay. The essay is organized according to the outline for the case study that was described earlier. Table 3.4 shows the proper organization and content that the case should contain. The outline appears in the left column, and the answer appears in the right column. Each part is explained to you.

Read Item 1 again carefully. You should notice that you're supposed to identify two strengths *and/or* needs. That's important information for how to structure the essay. What you will do is use the first two paragraphs of the essay, and the first sentence of the third paragraph, to answer Item 1 completely.

Structure and Function of Paragraphs 1 to 3.   The first paragraph of the essay states the first strength the data indicate. You include evidence to support your claim and where you found the information.

> The student's test data show that he can decode at grade level. This means that he reads with adequate fluency and accuracy and that he should have enough attention available to try to comprehend what he is reading.

In the second paragraph, you state the second strength.

> The teacher/student dialogue, his writing sample, and his test scores show that he does comprehend what he read literally. For example, he is able to identify factual information from the teacher's oral questions, and he can even summarize these ideas in writing.

Finally, the first sentence of the third paragraph conveys the major problem that the students is having.

> However, the student has a major problem with inferential comprehension, since he could not infer the problem that the main character is having with the fact that his cousin is coming over during the Super Bowl.

To this point, you have satisfied all of the principal parts of Item 1: to locate strengths and/ or needs in the data. Before you can answer Items 2 and 3 that ask for the lesson plans and the benefits, you have to finish the third paragraph. It serves a specific function, so pay careful attention to the next discussion.

The Structure and Function of Paragraph 3.   Let's look at the next two item statements to make sure that we are on track.

- Item 2:   Write two lesson plans for this student.
- Item 3:   Explain how these lesson plans will help the student's development.

Remember that the first sentence of Paragraph 3 states the student's major problem. Since the major problem is with inferential comprehension of narrative text, your next task is to identify and state two related needs for fluent decoding reflected in the data. These needs are in comprehending higher-level vocabulary words and in monitoring his understanding as he is reading. The reason that you must identify two "smaller" needs to the big "problem" is that Paragraph 3 is really an outline for Paragraphs 4 and 5. You are going to use Paragraphs 4 and 5 to answer Items 2 and 3.

To establish the outline, you simply state two small needs (subneeds) present in the data that are related to this major problem of fluent decoding. In this case, the two needs (A and B) that are related to fluent decoding are found in the balance of Paragraph 3.

- Need A: This may be because he has no strategies available to him to comprehend higher-level vocabulary words such as "mortified."
- Need B: Also, he may not have any strategies that will help him to make inferences as he reads text.

Again, establishing this outline in Paragraph 3 is essential for answering the two remaining item statements in the rest of the essay.

Structure and Function of Paragraphs 4 and 5.   To answer Item 2 (for example, two instructional designs) and Item 3 (for example, two benefits of these designs) of the case study question, you are going to use Paragraphs 4 and 5 of the essay. The topic sentences for each of these paragraphs are taken from the smaller needs that you identified in the third paragraph. You are going to write two separate lesson plans for them and then state the benefits of these lessons. Turning now to Paragraph 4, let's look at the opening sentence carefully.

> To help the student comprehend higher-level vocabulary words, the teacher should combine structural analysis with contextual analysis.

This sentence in Paragraph 4 simply restates Need A from Paragraph 3. Next, the essay includes the first instructional activity that you must state for Item 2.

> First, she should build on his syllabication strengths and teach him how to analyze the syllables for prefixes, suffixes, and roots. Then, the student should practice this strategy on selected words to ensure that he can do it. Next, the teacher should show the student how to reassemble the word and check the context of the sentence to confirm the meaning of the word.

Finally, Paragraph 4 closes with the first benefit that you must identify for Item 3.

> These activities would help the student to comprehend unfamiliar vocabulary words and would greatly increase his chances to comprehend text inferentially.

At this point, you have provided one required instructional activity and one required benefit. You are halfway through completing Items 2 and 3 of the case study.

To complete the rest of the case study, you'll be using the fifth paragraph. Like Paragraph 4, Paragraph 5 restates a need from Paragraph 3 (in this case, it is Need B):

> The student also needs to learn how to use self-questioning to make inferences while he reads.

This is followed by the second required instructional design.

> The teacher should use the passage and model how to ask questions during the reading. For example, she could model how to ask, "What is Martin like? Is Bob really happy about his coming over? Why does the last sentence say that this is the worst possible time for Martin to come to stay?"

The last task is to identify a related benefit of the activity that you have prescribed. The last sentence of the paragraph accomplishes that task.

> Learning how to ask and answer these questions will help the student to make inferences as he is reading the text.

At last! You have completed the three required tasks in the case study assignment using a five-paragraph essay. You identified two strengths in the first two paragraphs. You identified a major problem in the first sentence of Paragraph 3, along with two smaller needs. You identified two instructional activities related to the major identified need in Paragraphs 4 and 5. Finally, you identified two benefits related to the instructional designs that you wrote up in the final sentences of Paragraphs 4 and 5.

The essay format that you have just seen is the best method for writing any case study. You can easily adapt the activities from Chapter 2 to Paragraphs 4 and 5 of the case study. The next type of essay is the lesson plan. The sections that follow cover two different lessons, one for decoding and another for comprehension. Again, you will see how valuable the Chapter 2 activities and their formats really are in the next discussion.

WRITING LESSON PLANS FOR DECODING

The decoding model discussed in Chapter 2 is very helpful for analyzing data to reveal decoding problems. Table 3.5 shows the areas of the model that you should know by now.

You have to understand all of the aspects that lie behind each of the areas of the model. Furthermore, you may have to analyze data sets and write special lesson plans to help a child overcome some difficulty related to decoding. Since spelling may also be on the exam, let's look at a question and data that are related to that area of decoding as well.

> Based on your analysis of the spelling data, write an essay that demonstrates the following. First, state the need reflected in the data. Second, describe instruction to remedy the need you have identified. Third, state the benefit of the instruction you described.

You have three tasks to complete in this essay. First, you identify a need seen in the student's data (presented next). Second, you create a lesson plan that helps the student overcome the difficulty that she is having. Finally, you describe the benefit of the activity that you have identified. As you saw with the case study, to receive full credit, you must not only identify all three elements correctly, but also organize the answers such that evaluators can find them quickly and unmistakably. (*Note:* Objectives and prior assessment are omitted from this lesson plan and the one for comprehension, because the question does

TABLE 3.5   Overview of Decoding Instruction

FIRST: FOUNDATIONS OF DECODING		SECOND: EXPLICIT DECODING INSTRUCTION		THIRD: ULTIMATE AIM
Concepts about print	Phonemic awareness	Phonics skills	Sight words	Automatic decoding

DEVELOPMENTAL SPELLING INSTRUCTION (K–8)

not call for one. If your question asks you to define a learning objective on the test, make sure that you include one.)

    DATA SET FOR DECODING
- Spelling Items: cat   rat   hat   mat   sat
- Child's spelling: kt   rt   ht   mt   st

Since the question is related to spelling, it will be helpful if you take the time to memorize the components of spelling instruction that are tested on the exam. Table 3.6 is taken from Chapter 2.

    Based on the criteria in the table, the child is currently at the phonetic stage of spelling. Your task is to write a lesson plan to help the child transition from this stage into the conventional stage. This requires you to know appropriate activities for this need. Table 3.7 shows a sample answer to the question.

TABLE 3.6 Spelling Development

PRE-PHONETIC	PHONETIC	TRANSITIONAL	CONVENTIONAL
Scribbling	Encoding initial and final consonants	Encoding all sounds	Derivational spelling

TABLE 3.7 Example Answer to the Decoding Question

FORM	CONTENT
■ Need	The spelling data reflect that the child is in the phonetic stage. While able to encode initial and final consonants of words, she is not yet able to encode words using common rime patterns.
■ Lesson plan	Strategy: Begin by focusing on easily encoded words with common rimes (e.g., *mat, sat, hat,* etc.). **Materials:** Magnetic letters: B, C, H, M, R, S, Magnetic letter combination: AT White board Dry erase pen **Steps:** **1.** Distribute letters to the child and read each one aloud together, including the rime *-at.* **2.** Tell the child, "I want you to put one letter in front of *-at* and read the word." **3.** Work together to make words until each of the letters is used. **4.** Leave the consonant letters above the white board and write the rime *-at* on the board. **5.** Ask the student to write as many *-at* words beneath the rime as she can from memory, using the consonants as prompts.
■ Benefit	This lesson will help the child begin to encode medial and final sounds heard in words because she has been taught to write words by a common word family.

As the sample answer shows, you use three paragraphs for the essay. The first paragraph takes care of the need that the question requires. The second paragraph poses the instructional design that the question requests. Finally, the required benefit is stated in the third and last paragraph. Each paragraph is explained next in detail.

Paragraph 1: The Need

The first paragraph of the lesson plan is for the need.

> The spelling data reflect that the child is in the phonetic stage. While able to encode initial and final consonants of words, she is not yet able to encode words using common rime patterns.

It is important that you identify the correct need in the data so that you do not go off in a misdirection for the rest of the essay. Study the content of Chapter 2 carefully and know the models well to avoid such a problem.

Paragraph 2: The Lesson

The second paragraph of the essay describes the lesson plan that you will use to help the child with the need that you have identified. Because it is a spelling problem that is best addressed through a hands-on activity before practicing how to write the words, develop a lesson design in the following way. First, state the focus of lesson:

> Strategy: Begin by focusing on easily encoded words with common rimes. Second, state the materials to be used.
>
> Magnetic letters: B, C, H, M, R, S,
> Magnetic letter combination: AT
> White board
> Dry erase pen

Third, list steps to be carried out. Be sure that your steps follow a pattern that uses preplanning, teacher modeling, guided practice, and independent practice.

PREPLANNING
1. Distribute letters to the child and read each one aloud together, including the rime -*at*.
2. Tell the child, "I want you to put one letter in front of -*at* and read the word."

TEACHER MODELING
3. Work together to make words, until each of the letters is used.

GUIDED PRACTICE
4. Leave the consonant letters above the white board and write the rime -*at* on the board.

INDEPENDENT PRACTICE
5. Ask the student to write as many -*at* words beneath the rime as she can from memory, using the consonants as prompts.

Finally, since this is a spelling problem, the final step is to have the child write out the words. This pattern is appropriate for *all* lesson plans that are used to address student needs.

Paragraph 3: The Benefit

The final paragraph answers Item 3 by stating the benefit of the activity for this particular need.

> This lesson will help the child begin to encode medial and final sounds heard in words because she has been taught to write words by a common word family.

The key to writing these lesson plans is alignment: You must weave each part of their answer together such that the benefit aligns with the lesson plan to correct the need. Lack of alignment may result in a lowered score. In short, the need, lesson plan, and benefit must line up perfectly. The same type of format for the lesson plan is also appropriate for other areas of need, as the next example shows.

WRITING LESSON PLANS FOR COMPREHENSION

Comprehension questions are likely to be taken from Levels 3 and 4 of the model. They are reflected in Table 3.8.

TABLE 3.8 Levels 3 and 4

Level Three: Fluency

Level Four: Comprehension (Third Grade through Eighth Grade)

■ Vocabulary instruction	■ Literal, inferential, and evaluative comprehension	■ Pre-, while-, and post-reading strategies	■ Schema strategies

Be sure that you know each area of the table well and the activities that accompany each area. Here is an example of a comprehension-related question.

> Based on your analysis of the teacher and student conversation, write an essay that demonstrates the following. First, state the need reflected in the data. Second, describe instruction to remedy the need you have identified. Third, state the benefit of the instruction you described.

As in the previous question, you have three tasks in making your response. First, you identify a need that is present in the student's data. Second, you create a lesson plan that helps the student overcome the difficulty that she is having. Finally, you describe the benefit of the activity that you have identified.

To answer this particular comprehension question, you have to analyze data.

DATA SET FOR COMPREHENSION QUESTION
Did you know that the ocean stays warm long into the night? You might think that it is because the sun shines on it all day, which makes it hot. But even on cool and cloudy days, the ocean's temperature can still be warm after dark. How can that be?

The reason is that the sun's light is made up of waves. The waves are neither hot nor cold. The light waves penetrate the surface of the ocean and charge it, much like a battery. At night, the ocean releases all of the energy that it has been storing all day long. That's what makes the water feel warm at night.

TEACHER–STUDENT DIALOGUE

Teacher: Can you tell me what you were reading about?
Student: It's about the ocean.
Teacher: What does it say about the ocean?
Student: It says that it stays hot long into the night.
Teacher: Does it tell you why it stays hot all night?
Student: Yes. It says that the sun shines on it all day and that it heats up the water.
Teacher: Can you read this part for me (third sentence of second paragraph)?
Student: "The light waves penetrate the surface of the ocean and charge it, much like a battery." Oh, maybe it is something else that makes the ocean stay warm at night.

As you can see, this is expository text. Expository text is filled with factual items that must be understood both literally and inferentially. Since the child can answer the teacher's factual questions about the passage, you need to check to see how well the child can handle the teacher's inferential inquiries. It is apparent from the child's last statement that even she recognizes that she did not understand the inferred meanings of the text. The lesson plan that you write must address this need specifically. Table 3.9 shows an example answer to the question.

This response requires a need, a lesson plan, and a benefit. Following is an analysis of each paragraph.

Paragraph 1: The Need

The first paragraph focuses on the need and satisfies part one of the question.

> The student is able to comprehend expository text literally but not inferentially, because she did not understand that the sun charges the ocean like a battery at night, which causes it to stay warm after dark (she thought that the water just stayed warm).

The section on reading comprehension in Chapter 2 covers information relating to comprehending expository text, both literally and inferentially. Refer to that section for further clarification if you need it.

Paragraph 2: The Lesson

The second paragraph of this essay describes a think aloud that is meant to help the child acquire inferential comprehension. It describes how a teacher explicitly models the behavior that the child must adopt, along with how to move on to teacher/student practice. The lesson ends with the student practicing alone.

PREPLANNING

1. Model the process of making inferences using a passage and reveal your thinking process to the student.

TABLE 3.9   Example Answer to the Comprehension Question

FORM	CONTENT
▪ Need	The student is able to comprehend expository text literally but not inferentially, because she did not understand that the sun charges the ocean like a battery at night, which causes it to stay warm after dark (she thought that the water just stayed warm).
▪ Scaffolding lesson plan	Strategy: Begin by focusing on how to use details from the text as the basis for making inferences.

Steps:

1. Model the process of making inferences using a passage and reveal your thinking process to the student.
2. Show the student how to focus on the details of the text to create mental pictures of what the text is saying (How is the ocean like a battery? Why is that detail important?).
3. Continue posing questions to the passage that move into deeper inferences (If the ocean is like a battery, what happens to the energy that it collects?).
4. Work together with the student to assemble evidence to support the inferences you've been making.
5. Select a passage that requires making inferences and have the student practice the technique on the passage.

▪ Benefit	This activity would help the student improve her inferential comprehension of expository text because she would learn to use details from the text to make logical inferences about its meaning.

TEACHER MODELING

2. Show the student how to focus on the details of the text to create mental pictures of what the text is saying (How is the ocean like a battery? Why is that detail important?).
3. Continue posing questions to the passage that move into deeper inferences (If the ocean is like a battery, what happens to the energy that it collects?).

GUIDED PRACTICE

4. Work together with the student to assemble evidence to support the inferences you've been making.

INDEPENDENT PRACTICE

5. Select a passage that requires making inferences and have the student practice the technique on the passage.

Paragraph 3: The Benefit

The final paragraph of the sample essay states the benefit of the activity proposed for the need.

This activity would help the student improve her inferential comprehension of expository text because she would learn to use details from the text to make logical inferences about its meaning.

In sum, the structure of the third essay is the same as the first one, and all of the items must align or you will receive a lower score. All of the Chapter 2 activities and their structures for comprehension instruction lend themselves to these essays, regardless of whether you target comprehension levels, comprehension strategies, or text organization.

A PROCEDURAL ESSAY FOR A CLOZE ACTIVITY

Procedural essays may appear on the exam. These essay questions ask you to demonstrate that you understand how to state the steps for an assessment or an instructional activity. It is critical that you know all of the assessments for early decoding, along with all of the lessons that are used from decoding to oral and written language. In short, you need to know the procedures for everything that Chapter 2 covers. Selected focus questions on writing procedural essays appear at the end of this section to help you learn that material.

The following is an example of an essay that requires a procedural essay format.

A fifth-grade teacher wishes to increase his students' knowledge and awareness of a grammar point, specifically when to use the article *a* and the article *an* in English (e.g., *a* car v. *an* apple). Describe a procedure or instructional activity to accomplish this goal.

The question asks you to "describe a procedure or instructional activity to accomplish this goal." Since the question has the word *procedure* in it, you can easily identify the essay format that is required. Table 3.10 shows an example answer to the question.

Although only one paragraph in length, the essay is organized into three parts. Each part is discussed briefly.

TABLE 3.10   Procedural Essay Answer

FORM	CONTENT
■ What	A cloze activity can accomplish this goal. Here are the steps:
■ How (steps)	**1.** Construct a passage that has sentences with an equal number of nouns that begin with consonants and vowels. **2.** Put a blank line in front of each of the nouns in each sentence of the paragraph. **3.** Teach the rule that when a noun begins with a consonant, the article *a* is correct; if it begins with a vowel, use *an*. **4.** Distribute the passage and have students work in small groups to supply the correct article before the noun. **5.** Review the passage together. **6.** Ask the students to write the rule for when to use the articles *a* and *an* before nouns beginning with either a consonant or vowel.
■ Benefit	This activity will help students to understand proper article placement because they have learned and applied the rule.

Part 1

The first part of the essay simply states the tool or activity that you would use. In this case, a cloze activity is selected: "A cloze activity can accomplish this goal. Here are the steps." The sentence should be brief and use the appropriate "jargon" if possible (for example, a *cloze* activity).

Part 2

The second part of the essay states the steps that you would take to carry out the activity. The structure follows a logical order. The first and second steps demonstrate how you would construct the passage that will illustrate the grammar point that you want to illustrate. In the third step, you state that you will be teaching the grammar point explicitly. The fourth step has the students working independently. Finally, the fifth and sixth steps state that you will review the passage to ensure understanding. Notice that when stating steps, you can simply head each sentence with a verb (for example, *construct, put*). This will save your having to use unnecessary words and keep your essay within the fifty-word range. Plus, you'll be able to write the essay more quickly.

Part 3

The final part of this procedural essay conveys the benefit in one direct sentence. Simply put, you state that the activity will meet the goal the question requires and how the activity will accomplish it: "This activity will help students to understand proper article placement because they have learned and applied the rule."

The Chapter 2 formats make writing procedural essays quite easy since procedural questions really are needs-based lesson plans without the need or are descriptions of assessment or classroom planning procedures (selecting texts, arranging centers, planning units, or adapting instruction for special populations). The last type of essay is the justification, which can be applied to all areas of the model, too.

A JUSTIFICATION ESSAY FOR A RUNNING RECORD

Justification questions are another possibility on the test. In these, you are asked to state specific reasons why a particular assessment or instructional activity is valid. All areas of the model are fair game for these types of questions. Here is a sample justification question.

> A fourth-grade teacher determines a student's independent reading level by using a grade-level passage of 100 words. She has the student read aloud. As the student reads, she marks the words he omits, substitutes, and inserts. Then, she adds up the errors and subtracts them from 100. This calculation gives the correct reading level (e.g., 100–96 = independent; 95–90 = instructional; 89 or below = frustration).
>
> Using your knowledge of how to determine a student's independent reading level, write a response that justifies how this activity can help you to plan reading instruction for students.

To answer this question, you must understand how assessments to determine student independent reading levels work. In this case, the assessment tool in question is an informal reading inventory, which is discussed in Level 1 of the model from Chapter 2. Table 3.11 shows the form and content appropriate to satisfy the question.

TABLE 3.11 Justification Essay Example

FORM	CONTENT
■ What ■ Why ■ Benefit	Informal reading inventories and running records can tell you whether the child is reading at grade level. As the child reads aloud, you mark the student's performance to determine whether the child relies on visual information, grammatical information, or meaning. This will inform where you need to begin instruction. Finally, knowing the student's independent reading level will tell you the appropriate grade level from which to draw texts for this student to read independently during sustained silent reading, read aloud to other students, or read at home with parents.

The form of this justification essay follows a predictable pattern. Each sentence and its function are presented next.

Sentence 1

The first sentence conveys that you know what the tool is and what it tells you: "Informal reading inventories and running records can tell you whether the child is reading at grade level." Clearly, you must know your assessment tools to pass this test.

Sentences 2 and 3

The next two sentences state why the tool works and why a teacher would use it: "As the child reads aloud, you mark the student's performance to determine whether the child relies on visual information, grammatical information, or meaning as they read. This will inform where you need to begin instruction."

Sentence 4

The final sentence closes with the benefit of this activity: "Finally, knowing the student's independent reading level will tell you the appropriate grade level from which to draw texts for this student to read independently during sustained silent reading, read aloud to other students, or read at home with parents."

In addition to knowing the steps and procedures for the activities in Chapter 2, be sure that you understand the philosophy that stands behind the assessment or activity. This will make writing justification essays much easier.

CONCLUSION

The written section of the test is the easiest portion to control. The most important thing that you can do to increase your chances of reaching your magic score is to do well on the writing. The forms that you have learned about in this chapter will help you to organize your answers quickly and effectively. Furthermore, if you take the time to learn the content from Chapter 2, the forms will be pretty simple for you to fill in. The best advice is to re-write the essays that you have seen in this chapter a few times. Then, go through Chapter 2 and write procedural and justification essays for the major parts of the model. Doing so will help you to write answers to these types of questions with ease. This preparation will also help you to answer multiple-choice questions since many of the very same patterns are used to structure the questions. You can pick out answers much more easily if you know these forms. Plus, you must learn the content of Chapter 2, and Chapter 6 ensures that you will through writing and other activities.

CHAPTER FOUR

MAGIC BUBBLES

This chapter focuses on handling the multiple-choice questions that you are most likely to encounter about the model described in Chapter 2. You are really going to need strategies to survive this section. The types of strategies that you need are twofold. First, you need to know ways to make the multiple-choice questions work for you. This chapter discusses what that means after you have taken the diagnostic test. Second, you need to understand how to analyze the questions using the information from Chapter 2. If you only read Chapter 2 but do not perform any writing, the information may wash over you. That is why the text advises all candidates to read Chapter 3, even if not all their tests include essays. Taking this approach shows you how to actively learn the information in Chapter 2 through Chapter 6 and the appendices.

You also need the study guides that may be available for your exam. See your official registration bulletin for the order form or visit http://www.ablongman.com\boosalis for links to your state's department of education for downloading instructions. Restrictions may apply to who is allowed to order or download these materials, so read any printed or online disclaimers before attempting to obtain the information.

DIAGNOSTIC TEST

Before learning how to do the multiple-choice questions on the exam, take the diagnostic test that follows. You need to time yourself for this test. Before you start the test, get a timer and set it for six minutes. See how far you get.

A fourth-grade student named Chris reads the passage below with appropriate fluency and accuracy.

Why do some people do unhealthy things? Some people keep smoking, even though they know that it will kill them. "I just kept on smoking," said Tom, "I knew that it was harmful to me, but I just could not stop. I could feel it hurting my lungs, not to mention how it made my clothes smell. But I smoked anyway. I had to find a new set of rewards to make myself quit."

The reason that some people find it hard to change habits is because of conditioning. Conditioning happens when we associate a behavior with something else. For example, Tom might associate smoking with relaxation, and any time that he feels stress, he might smoke to relieve that stress. The danger is that many of these conditioned behaviors are harmful to us and can be very hard to change. As Tom said, he continued to smoke, even though he knew that it was bad for him. To quit, he had to *recondition* himself to associate pleasure with something other than smoking.

> **Teacher:** Tell me what you were reading about.
>
> **Chris:** It's about Tom. He used to smoke.
>
> **Teacher:** Does it say why he smoked?
>
> **Chris:** It says that he doesn't know why he smoked.
>
> **Teacher:** Does it say why he quit smoking?
>
> **Chris:** Yes. He wanted to get into better physical conditioning.

1. Which of the following areas best describes Chris's need in reading comprehension?

   A. Literal comprehension of expository text
   B. Inferential comprehension of expository text
   C. Fluent decoding of polysyllabic words
   D. Sequencing details from a grade-level passage

2. Which of the following activities would characterize the best approaches to take next to target Chris's need in reading comprehension?

   I. A semantic features analysis of homophones
   II. A think-aloud activity to help Chris self-regulate his comprehension while reading
   III. A choral-reading activity for fluency
   IV. A sequencing activity for expository text

   A. I only
   B. II and III
   C. I, II, and IV
   D. II and IV

3. A first-grade teacher is planning a big book activity for her students. First, she selects the text and gathers the materials that will be required for the activity. She decides to use an easel and a pointer for the activity. Since the students have been working on big book readings for several weeks now, she decides to let the children take a direct role in the activity. After deciding to have the children take turns identifying the parts of a book,

including the cover, the title, and the author's name, she considers what to do next. Which of the following items best reflects what the students could do next?

A. React and comment on specific parts of the text that the teacher will preselect
B. Review the story's components (setting, purpose, etc.) after it has been read
C. Demonstrate their knowledge of the correct direction in which to read
D. Discuss the type of text that was read

4. A kindergarten teacher writes the following sentence on the board:

Today is Friday, September 29, 2003.

She then reads the passage to the students, pointing to each word as she reads. Next, she reads the passage aloud with the children, pointing to each word as the group reads together. Using your knowledge of early reading activities, which response best represents the skill that the teacher is targeting?

A. Reading text with proper intonation and fluency
B. Understanding that individual letters represent individual sounds
C. Recognizing that days of the week should be capitalized
D. Understanding direction in which text is read in English

ANSWERS

1. B, 2. D, 3. C, 4. D.

SELF-ASSESSMENT

How did you do? How much time did you take? More importantly, *what did you do on the questions?* Let's see if you fell victim to any of the following traps.

1. You did the questions in order.
2. You spent longer than two minutes per question.
3. You read the reading passage first before reading the multiple-choice question for questions 1 and 2.
4. You couldn't do the question with the Roman numerals in it quickly—or at all.
5. You didn't do question 4 first.
6. You didn't write on the test.

If you answered "yes" to any question above, you might be at risk of having to repeat the exam. A full discussion of why these pitfalls are so hazardous is next.

DISCUSSION

Doing the questions in order and spending longer than two minutes per question are traps that many unsuccessful candidates fall into. These are traps because you lose valuable opportunities to do easy questions (called "gimmies") and questions that are actually scored. Worse, you lose a great deal of time if you don't know how to work through questions efficiently. Time is often a great killer on these tests, which is especially true of the multiple-choice section. Essentially, every second counts here, and you cannot afford to waste a moment.

Since you probably cannot expect to do the questions in order, you must use methods and strategies to help you to skip through the exam effectively on your way to a passing score. You also need to manage your time as you work through the exam strategically. If you spent longer than two minutes per question, you probably committed the third error: reading the data first. This is also a very harmful trap. Nothing eats up more time on any test than trying to figure out student data sets. Again, you may need strategies to get through these types of questions, the first of which is simply forcing yourself to read the test questions before looking at the data. That may take some concentration since it is so tempting to read whatever happens to be next in line on the multiple-choice section.

If the question with Roman numerals gave you trouble, it is because you lack skills in this area. You may not have written on your test, either. While these types of questions may not be on the exam, the odds are that you will have to complete some pretty odd-looking questions. Plus, all of the questions require some degree of "figuring." To complete questions on any exam, expect to mark up your test. Just think of it as writing your way to a passing score.

Given this discussion, think about how you really performed on the four questions now. Even if you got all of them correct, reconsider how you arrived at those answers since you may be falling into traps that result in you repeating the test.

The remainder of this chapter shows you effective methods for doing the multiple-choice items strategically. The remaining sections of this chapter show you how to use the tables from Appendix A effectively for all questions related to the model in Chapter 2.

At this time, you should at least begin your search for the study guides applicable to your exam. These study guides may be available from the company and from the department of education in your state. The only multiple-choice materials that this text recommends you use are the ones that come directly from the company. Any other materials represent someone's best guess at what the items will look like, which is insufficient for the level of practice required here. It may also be harmful since you may grow accustomed to using materials that do not align to the exam. Obtain the study guides to ensure that you have undertaken proper practice.

MULTIPLE-CHOICE STRATEGIES

The four most important strategies are described next. They help you to work through the exam effectively so that you are not tripped up on the exam or on questions that do not count.

1. Read the question item first. If you took the time to read the reading passage on bad habits and the teacher/student dialogue prior to reading the first two questions, you yourself have a bad habit in need of change. The first thing to do is to read the question, not the data! This is because you have to know what you're reading the data for. Plus, you have to decide if you're going to bother doing the question right away or save it for later or guess on it toward the end (yes, you'll be answering every question, but some items might be done with a simple "bubble"). Question 1 is about the type of comprehension that the student lacks. After reading the question, review the teacher/student dialogue first, and then test the student's responses against the passage. Try that technique now. You'll find that it takes you only seconds to understand that the child cannot comprehend expository text inferentially. This technique alone may save you an infinite amount of time on the actual test.

2. Do the Roman numeral questions strategically. Roman numeral questions, like question 2 in the diagnostic test, require strategies. Reread the question from the diagnostic test:

Which of the following activities would characterize the best approaches to take next to target Chris's need in reading comprehension?

I.   A semantic features analysis of homophones
II. A think-aloud activity to help Chris self-regulate his comprehension while reading
III. A choral-reading activity for fluency
IV. A sequencing activity for expository text

A. I only
B. II and III
C. I, II and IV
D. II and IV

Here is the explanation for how to do them (NESINC, 2001).

First, read each of the Roman numeral items, underlining the key words in each statement.

I.   A semantic features analysis of homophones
II. A think-aloud activity to help Chris self-regulate his comprehension while reading
III. A choral-reading activity for fluency
IV. A sequencing activity for expository text

Second, eliminate the Roman numeral items that obviously will not work. Those items include anything that will not work for ~~literal~~ *inferential* comprehension of expository text.

I.   ~~A semantic features analysis of homophones~~
II. A think-aloud activity to help Chris self-regulate his comprehension while reading
III. ~~A choral-reading activity for fluency~~
IV. A sequencing activity for expository text

Third, turn to the answers and eliminate the responses that contain the items that you've eliminated from the list.

~~A. I only~~
~~B. II and III~~
~~C. I, II and IV~~
D. II and IV

A, B, and C are eliminated because they contain the items eliminated from the Roman numeral items. This leaves D as the only correct response.

3. Identify gimmies, 50/50s, and "Letter C" questions. Plan on skipping around on the test (explained in Chapter 5). The reason is that you do not want to miss the gimmies! Question 4 is one that you should have done first. It is short, easy (if you know the content of Chapter 2), and might otherwise be missed if you're not working the test efficiently. 50/50s are questions in which you can eliminate only a couple of possible answers. Work on those questions only after you've nailed the gimmies (question 3 might be like that for you). "Letter C" questions are ones that you're never going to get, no matter what you do. If you can't understand the question or cannot eliminate any possible answers, then skip it. Go back later and use your favorite letter and guess. My favorite letter is *C,* because *C* is for *Chris.* You are on your own for guessing, though. (*Note:* Many students find that using the same letter consistently when guessing is more effective than trying to "guess around" with a variety of letters.)

4. Be sure that you know your magic score and complete those multiple-choice questions with care—then guess away if time grows very short. If your test has an essay section, you should emerge from the writing with a good number of points. Following the methods for the essay questions in Chapter 3 helps you achieve that goal. Doing so reduces the number of multiple-choice questions that you have to answer correctly. If your test contains only multiple-choice questions, you are going to have to exercise more care on this section and be sure you know how many questions need careful consideration and how many do not.

The next section shows you how to use the models that you learned about in Chapter 2 to answer multiple-choice questions.

USING THE TABLES TO ANSWER MULTIPLE-CHOICE QUESTIONS

The tables from Chapter 2 are extremely useful when answering multiple-choice questions. That is why Chapter 2 looks as it does and why Appendix A has tables for you to complete and use in your studies and on the test. The questions may ask you what you should do first, next, or last in terms of assessment and instruction. The easiest way to manage such questions is to have the model or reading instruction in mind, along with knowing each component. As you recall, there are six basic areas, shown in Table 4.1, that are assessed in concepts about print, and teachers use a particular order when assessing children.

TABLE 4.1   Concepts about Print

Parts of a book	Print carries meaning	Tracking print	Words in sentences	Letters within words	Upper- and lowercase letters names

Knowing both the components of concepts about print and the order of assessment is important for certain types of questions on the test.

A kindergarten student demonstrates that she can easily locate the cover and title of a book. Which of the following areas should the teacher assess next?

A. Whether the child can locate words within sentences
B. Whether the child can track print one to one
C. Whether the child can name the upper- and lowercase letters
D. Whether the child knows where to start reading

Using the table, it is easy to see and understand why D is the best response. Knowing where to start reading is the same as indicating that print carries meaning, so D is the correct response. The same idea holds true for concepts about print activities: You may be asked what purposes morning messages and big book readings serve in instructing early literacy. To answer these questions, you have to know the activities in Chapter 2.

The tables from Chapter 2 also are helpful for you if you are asked to diagnose needs in student data. Following is an example from spelling.

A child writes the following sentence during a language experience activity:

Te cat iz hr tda (The cat is here today.)

Which of the following best reflects the child's current stage of spelling?

A. Pre-phonetic
B. Orthographic
C. Phonetic
D. Transitional

In the section on spelling development, Table 4.2 was offered to illustrate each stage of spelling.

Analyzing the spelling data in the multiple-choice question is much easier when you have a frame of reference to work with. It is easy to see that the spellings are all phonetic, despite the correctly spelled sight word *cat*. Furthermore, you may be asked what appropriate action the teacher should take next to help this student improve in her spelling. The only way for you to answer that question, or to *find* the correct answer to that question, is

TABLE 4.2   Spelling Development

PRE-PHONETIC	PHONETIC	TRANSITIONAL	CONVENTIONAL
I ⊃≯ꝑ	Brd	braꝺe	"bread"

to recall the activities that move children from phonetic to transitional spelling. Again, knowing the content behind the table is critical for handling the multiple-choice section.

To meet the goal of learning the content of Chapter 2 as easily as possible, the best approach is to follow the study plan in Chapter 6. You study the content of Chapter 2 by using tables in Appendix A first (please skim them now). As you saw earlier in this chapter, these tables are very helpful for studying multiple-choice questions that target the model. Then, you read Chapter 3 to learn the correct essay formats for answering the questions in the study plan. You also learn your state's standards (Appendix B) and effective ways to analyze data (Appendix C). Virtually everything that you need to be successful on the test is here; all that you need to do is dedicate yourself to active study.

STUDY GUIDES

As discussed in the preface and at the beginning of this chapter, the best way to prepare for the multiple-choice questions on the test is to obtain the study guides for your test from the company itself. If you use materials other than the official samples, you risk practicing formats that do not parallel what you will actually see on the day of the test. That could be a very bad mistake. When you register for the exam, you should receive information about the study guides (if available) and how to purchase them. In addition, many study guides are available online at your state's education department. Visit http://www.ablongman.com/boosalis for the direct link. Restrictions may apply to who is allowed to download the information, so check the policies before attempting to acquire the information from the Internet.

CONCLUSION

The multiple-choice questions, like the essay questions, require strategies and a deep knowledge of the content of Chapter 2 for success. In the next chapter, you learn about how to manage the test as a whole, whether it is multiple-choice only or a written and multiple-choice exam, in order to reach your magic score.

CHAPTER FIVE

MAGIC MOMENTS: EFFECTIVE TIME MANAGEMENT METHODS

The first chapter of this book discusses the magic score required for your test. The magic score is the hidden raw score required to pass the test based on adding the score from each section together (if there are multiple sections). This chapter shows you how to manage your time on the test as a whole to achieve that magic score. You cannot afford to run out of time on the test because that is a major reason for failure among repeat test takers. Furthermore, if you use the methods described in this chapter, you can use the test itself to your own advantage in some cases.

These tests come in two major formats. The first format is the written exam with multiple-choice questions. The following sections describe several major methods for this format: the "One Pass" and "Two Step" approaches. Obviously, if your test is multiple-choice only, you can skip the information on the "One Pass" and "Two Step" models. However, all candidates need to read the plans for managing time on the multiple-choice sections, called "divide and conquer" and "seek and destroy." These models will help all candidates to handle these sections of the test effectively.

METHODS FOR WRITTEN EXAMS WITH MULTIPLE-CHOICE ITEMS

You'll have the option of using one of two primary time management methods: the "One Pass" or the "Two Step." A third model is offered after these major methods. Though all of these approaches are effective for helping you to obtain your magic score, each one serves a different purpose. You have the chance to choose the method that will work best for you, depending on what your situation is. If you are a slow reader, for example, one of the two methods might work better for you. Or, if you have no time to learn all of the content for the test, then another method might be a better choice. How to choose between methods is discussed in the last part of this section. Right now, let's look at the two best methods for managing time and getting your magic score.

THE "ONE PASS" METHOD

The method is termed *"One Pass"* because you do the written sections first in a specific order and leave the multiple-choice portion for last. The reason is simple. If you run low on time during the multiple-choice section, you can fill in the bubbles with your number 2 pencil, using your favorite letter consistently (see Chapter 4). Think about it. Getting the written questions out of the way first allows you to spend more time working the multiple choice strategically. And, if you have to rush through the multiple-choice questions, you can. But if you do the test in the reverse, you can't just "bubble in" the written sections. This may be the biggest mistake that students commit when taking the test the first time— and many people continue to repeat the same error into their sixth and seventh attempts. There is a something to be learned from these unsuccessful experiences.

Since the California RICA is the largest and most challenging of all of these exams, let's see how "One Pass" applies to this test. There is a written portion with one case study, four short answers, and seventy multiple-choice items (only sixty count). Four hours are available for the test. The magic score on this exam is 81. See Table 5.1.

TABLE 5.1 "One Pass" Method

	WRITTEN				MULTIPLE CHOICE
First	*Second*	*Third*	*Fourth*	*Fifth*	*Last*
Case study	Short answer 2	Short answer 3	Short answer 4	Short answer 1	Multiple-choice section
24 points	12 points	12 points	6 points	6 points	60 points
60 min.	20 min.	20 min.	10 min.	10 min.	120 min.

Using "One Pass," a candidate knocks out the written sections first. The initial questions that you answer are the ones that value the most points. Those essays happen to include the case study and short answers 2 and 3. Regardless of the order in which the test is given, you do the case study first, the two essays that value the most points next, and the essays that value the least points last. The remaining time is spent working the multiple-choice section strategically.

WHAT ARE THE BENEFITS OF "ONE PASS"?

The main benefit of "One Pass" is that is helps you to manage time and to nail the essays that value the most points before attempting the multiple-choice section. It is also very straightforward and works best for students who want a simple time management model to work with. There are some cautions, however. If your knowledge of reading instruction content is weak, or if it appears that you do not have time to prepare for the test, then "One Pass" might not be for you. Instead, you need to rely on the method described next because

TABLE 5.2   "Two Step" Method: Part One

First step: Outline the case study and/or the short-answer questions, and then complete the multiple-choice items.

First outline case study	Second, outline SA 1	Third, outline SA 2	Fourth outline SA 3	Fifth, outline SA 4	Sixth, do multiple-choice
■ Strength	■ Need	■ Need	■ What	■ How	
■ Strength	■ Lesson	■ Lesson	■ Steps	■ What	
■ Problem	■ Benefit	■ Benefit	■ Benefit	■ Benefit	
■ Lesson					
■ Lesson					
		15 min.			120 min.

it is for students who might need additional support during the exam to reach their magic score.

THE "TWO STEP" METHOD

The "Two Step" is an alternative method of presentation that is also very effective. It is the preferred method for anyone who faces an exam with written and multiple-choice sections. There are two steps to the method. The first step is to survey and outline each of the essays and then do the multiple-choice questions for a defined amount of time. Table 5.2 shows an example for a four-hour exam with a case study, four short answers, and seventy multiple choice items, like the California RICA.

After completing as many of the multiple-choice items that you can answer easily, you return to the essays and finish writing them. The answers are written according to the relative point values of the essays, as seen in "One Pass." See Table 5.3. If all of the essays are of equal value, then you do the easiest essay first. This way, you are sure to at least earn as many points as you can.

TABLE 5.3   "Two Step" Method: Part Two

Second step: Write the case study, short answers 2 and 3, then 1 and 4. Finish any remaining multiple-choice questions last.

Seventh, write the case study (24 points)	Eighth, write 12-point essay	Ninth, write 12-point essay	Tenth, write 6-point essay	Eleventh, write 6-point essay	Finish multiple-choice items
45 min.	20 min.	20 min.	10 min.	10 min.	remaining time

After writing the essays, if you have any time remaining, then you spend it guessing on multiple-choice items that you will never be able to answer, even if you have the best materials available in front of you.

WHAT ARE THE BENEFITS OF "TWO STEP"?

The multiple-choice questions may be packed with terms, activities, and content that could be useful to you. Because of the abundance of possible clues that might be contained in the multiple-choice questions, you may be able to actually use the test against itself. Perhaps surveying and outlining the essay questions first will allow you to "backfill" them with information pulled from the multiple-choice questions. If your knowledge of content is weak, you might want to use this approach, though we recommend it for everyone.

SHOULD I "ONE PASS" OR "TWO STEP"?

You know yourself best. Here are the criteria for each of these methods and who might benefit from using a particular method over another one. Consider using "One Pass" if both conditions apply to you.

1. You read and write slowly. It is geared for candidates who feel that they might need to stomp their way through the test toward a passing score.
2. Your knowledge of the content seems pretty stable. If you know your stuff, then use "One Pass." This is because you won't need to try to use the test against itself to answer any of the questions. And, since you know the material, use the easiest method for obtaining your magic score—and that's "One Pass." You'll get a sense of whether you know the content now that you have finished reading Chapter 2.

However, "Two Step" is by far the preferred method among the successful test takers we know. Here are the criteria for it.

1. You read efficiently and can manage your time effectively. If you have enough time to learn the time management strategies for "Two Step," then use it.
2. You find the content particularly baffling or simply don't have enough time to study the content for the test. In this case, you're going to have to get help during the test— and the test itself may be your best partner and study buddy. By sketching out the written questions first and then attempting to use the multiple-choice questions to supplement terms and activities within each outline, you may increase your chances of passing, even if your knowledge of content is totally absent.

"Two Step" is the preferred method. The sheer amount of information that the tests cover means that you're going to need all of the potential help you can get. Taking time to study the content contained in this book, while preparing to use the "Two Step" method, is a great recipe for success.

A FINAL WORD ABOUT METHODS

If you have enough time to prepare for the test, then try to remain as flexible as possible with your time. Review the methods thoroughly so that you become nimble enough to use a hybrid of these approaches if necessary. A hybrid simply means that you survey the written sections first, answer or outline the case study next, answer or outline short answers 2 and 3 after that, and then outline or answer short answers 1 and 4 last. After outlining or answering the written questions, you complete the multiple-choice questions, saving enough time to return to the short answers that you outlined only because you couldn't figure them out completely. The remaining time is spent filling in any written-response outlines with the information that you have "borrowed" from the multiple-choice questions.

Table 5.4 offers an example for you to use if you find yourself needing to use your own hybrid approach. It is based on a four-hour exam like the California RICA.

TABLE 5.4   Hybrid Approach

CASE STUDY	ESSAY 1	ESSAY 2	ESSAY 3	ESSAY 4	MULTIPLE CHOICE
60 min.	10 min.	20 min.	20 min.	10 min.	120 min.
Enter your time spent	Enter your time spent	Enter your time spent	Enter your time spent	Enter your time spent	Enter your time spent

The idea is that you scribble this table in your test book (if allowed) to keep track of your time as you take the test. It is your responsibility to figure out the times that are applicable for each section if you intend to use this model since it is impossible to predict whether the question will inspire only an outline from you and not a full response.

THE MULTIPLE-CHOICE STRATEGIES

If you ask, "Why do I need multiple-choice methods to manage time on this section?," just remember that you are trying to get a particular magic score on the exam and that the multiple-choice section may contain many pitfalls that stand between you and that goal (see Chapter 4). First of all, you may be asked more questions than are actually counted as Chapter 1 describes. For example, of seventy questions asked, only sixty of them are scored. If you cannot work efficiently, you might waste a great deal of time on questions that aren't even going to count in your favor. There is simply no way to speculate about which questions are real and which are not. Instead, you learn how to work through questions effectively so that the "empty questions" become a nonissue.

Recall also that question length and type may be another problem. For example, many questions might include data sets followed by questions about the data. Data sets might be teacher notes, teacher/student discussions, lengthy paragraphs, or student worksheets. It is very easy to get lost in the data sets and the questions, as Chapter 4 shows. Valuable time is lost. In short, you can expect to spend most of the two hours allotted for the multiple-choice section. Using methods and strategies, your time is well spent on your way to earning the most points possible.

In this section, you learn how to use two different time management methods to reach your magic score. Here is the rationale for each approach. You have to find a minimum number of questions that you can answer on the test. If you are fortunate to have a test that includes essays, you can reduce the number of multiple-choice questions that you have to be certain on. If not, then working the multiple-choice section effectively is critical. Try to get accustomed to the idea that you are *searching* the multiple-choice section *for those questions,* and not just doing the first item to the last one in order. Remember: There are items that aren't going to count and that are simply too long and complicated to bother with. As such, the next several sections show you two methods that will help you find the minimum number of questions required to pass.

THE "DIVIDE AND CONQUER" METHOD

Within the multiple-choice section, your goal is to nail a magic number of questions. This does not mean that you ignore the rest of the questions, though. You are answering all of the items since there is usually no penalty for guessing (consult your registration bulletin). "Divide and Conquer" is a reasonable method for identifying and answering questions strategically to ensure that you find those forty-plus questions. In short, you break the test up into sections and spend allotted amounts of time in them. Table 5.5 shows the breakdown for a seventy-item test such as the California RICA with a ~~four~~-hour maximum.

three

TABLE 5.5 "Divide and Conquer" Method

SECTION 1	SECTION 2	SECTION 3	SECTION 4	SECTION 5	SECTION 6	SECTION 7
Items 1–10	Items 10–20	Items 20–30	Items 30–40	Items 40–50	Items 50–60	Items 60–70
17 min.	17 min.	17 min.	17 min.	17 min.	17 min.	17 min.

Following are the steps for using "Divide and Conquer."

1. Divide the test into seven sections.
2. Spend no more than seventeen minutes per section.
3. Work within sections to read each question first and decide on the ones that are worth answering and on the ones that should be skipped for now.
4. Nail the "gimmies" within the section.
5. Do the questions that require some thought, paying careful attention to the time.
6. Move on to the next section and repeat steps 1 through 6.
7. Use your final five minutes of the exam to guess on the questions that you skipped entirely.

These strategies help you stay focused, avoid running out of time, and find the critical number of question that you need to pass the test.

BENEFITS AND CAUTIONS
OF "DIVIDE AND CONQUER"

The main benefit of "Divide and Conquer" is that it helps you to work through the exam efficiently. Many students who fail the exam on their first attempt (or on multiple attempts) probably could manage to do only half of the questions before having to guess on the remaining thirty questions because they ran out of time. This is a terrible strategy. "Divide and Conquer" helps you to focus your attention on ten questions at a time. You move through the exam, nailing the easy questions and then the ones that require a little bit of thought. You should quickly have the minimum number of questions that you need to pass. The only caution is to be careful when marking your answer sheet. Because you are skipping around on the sections, you have to be sure that you "bubble in" the right number on the answer sheet that corresponds to your question.

THE "SEEK AND DESTROY" METHOD

Another method of finding the minimum number of questions is called "Seek and Destroy." Here, you use the traditional approach of reading a question and deciding whether to answer it. Briefly, if it looks easy, then you attempt it; if not, you skip it. If you choose to skip a question, you write a check in the margin next to the question if it is one that you can get with just a little more time. If it is a real time waster, then you write a question mark. You move through items one through seventy, doing questions that you know, skipping questions that you don't know, and writing in the margins of the test. Once you reach the end of the exam, you return to the items that are checked and complete them. After finishing the checked items, you guess on the time wasters, using your favorite letter. "Seek and Destroy" is an adequate way to plod your way through the questions without having to read ahead as in "Divide and Conquer."

BENEFITS AND CAUTIONS OF "SEEK AND DESTROY"

The main benefit of this approach is that you do not have to read ahead. Many students who do not feel comfortable doing the test in sections may prefer this straightforward approach. You should find the minimum number of questions using this method, though you have to work within your own defined time limits. And that is the major caution: You have to work out your own time management plan to use this method. If you keep in mind that two minutes is about the most time that you can spend on any one question, you'll have some sense of what to do.

WHICH TIME MANAGEMENT METHOD
SHOULD I CHOOSE?

Choosing a method is simple: If you feel comfortable reading ahead and looking for questions within a section, "Divide and Conquer" is for you. If you do not feel comfortable with reading ahead, stick to "Seek and Destroy." "Divide and Conquer" is the preferred method because the times for each section are defined.

THE TIME MANAGEMENT METHODS ILLUSTRATED
FOR YOUR EXAM

The time management methods for both the written-response and multiple-choice sections of the exam are now applied to the specific tests that this book covers. These models are suggestions only, but they have earned high praise from many students who have found them to be instrumental in their success.

Since you cannot afford to run out of time on either the written or multiple-choice sections, the examples that follow use "Two Step" and "Divide and Conquer." If you do not like these methods, you must work out your own time plans for your test. Be sure that you have decided on the method that you are going to use prior to taking the exam.

Times are included in each illustration. These stated times are maximum times. You need to learn how to be aware of how much time you're spending on each section of the exam. During the actual session, gauge how well you're doing based on how much time you are allowed to spend on each part of the test. Draw a chart or a table on the scratch paper that you have and mark off each minute that you spend. Any time that you save on either section allows you to go back and guess on multiple-choice items that you couldn't figure out or check your grammar and spelling on the written portions.

California Reading Instruction Competence
Assessment (RICA)

MAGIC SCORE: 81 POINTS	
Written portion	**60 points**
Essay 1 (50 words)	6 points
Essay 2 (150 words)	12 points
Essay 3 (150 words)	12 points
Essay 4 (50 words)	6 points
Case study (300 words)	24 points
Multiple choice (70 items)	**60 points**

Source: RICA Registration Bulletin 2002–2003.

The RICA is a four-hour event. Expect to use all four hours of your time on this exam. The magic score on this exam is 81 out of 120 points. There are seventy multiple-choice items, but only sixty of them count. There are also four short-answer questions that range in value from 6 to 12 points. Finally, there is a case study that is worth 24 points. This adds up to a total of 120 points. Your goal is to get about 50 points on the written section and 45 on the multiple-choice section. That does not equal a grand total of 95. Remember that ten of the multiple-choice items are thrown out, so it might turn out to be an 85 (four more points than you need to pass this exam).

When you first sit down to take the test, survey the essays and the case (see the example in "Two-Step Method" earlier in this chapter). Then, write your outlines from Chapter 3. This should take you fifteen minutes. You have to study the content of Chapter 2 and memorize all of the forms in Chapter 3. These types of questions are on the exam in one form or another. After getting some sense of the written questions and figuring out your outlines, start the multiple-choice questions.

Work the multiple-choice section methodically (see the example in "Divide and Conquer" earlier in this chapter). Use "Divide and Conquer" to divide the test up into seven sections. Within each section, find the "gimmies" and the items that you can figure out with some effort. Leave the "time wasters" for last. Remember that you are trying to keep moving through each section as you saw in the "Divide and Conquer" section. You can spend only about 120 minutes on the multiple-choice section. Do not lose sight of the goal here: You are looking for forty-five questions that you can answer and be certain about. The remaining twenty-five questions are answered, but they are less important than these critical forty-five questions. It is likely that the forty-five questions that you can answer will be distributed throughout the exam rather than being "bunched up" in a couple of sections. This is why you have to keep flowing through the test. If you do not, you might end up guessing on the remaining twenty questions and needlessly miss easy points.

The next step is to return to the written questions and finish them (see the example in "Two Step Method" earlier in this chapter. Do the case study first, the two essays that are worth 12 points each next, and the two essays that are worth 6 points each last. Stay within the time limits described in the "Two Step" approach. Since you have the outlines ready, begin to fill them in on the test. You may be able to pull terms and activities from the multiple-choice section into these essays. Be careful with your spelling and grammar and be sure to write clearly. If you have to print each of these essays, then do it. That might just save your score.

Use any remaining time to guess on multiple-choice questions that you could not get or to check your grammar and spelling on the written questions. You should be able to reach your magic score in under four hours.

Arizona Educator Proficiency Assessments (AEPA)—Elementary Education (Reading)

MAGIC SCORE: 80 POINTS	
Essay 1 (300 words)	10 points
Multiple choice (100 items)	70 points

Source: AEPA Registration Bulletin (2002).

The passing score on the AEPA is a scaled score of 240 on a 100–300 point scale. You have four hours to get it. The magic score to keep in mind a raw score of 80 from a combined score on both sections. To get your magic score on the multiple-choice section alone, you will need to be sure on at least 85 questions, 15 items better than 70. Unfortunately, an unknown number of questions will be thrown out, so Arizona candidates will have to be even more careful with how they approach this section. The remaining points will be earned from the essay, where you will hopefully earn between 5 and 10 points. Keeping these numbers in mind will help you reach a magic score of 80, regardless of how many multiple-choice items are thrown out.

Here is how to get your magic score.

FIRST	SECOND	THIRD
Survey the essay question. Develop an outline.	Do the multiple-choice section. Spend no more than 16 minutes per section.	Complete the essay using terms and ideas from the multiple choice.
10 min.	160 min.	60 min.

Outline the essay first and then start working the multiple-choice items carefully over a 160-minute period. Try to nail the "gimmies" and work on the items that you can get with little effort. Skip the items that you're never going to get. Use your time as follows:

1–10	10–20	20–30	30–40	40–50	50–60	60–70	70–80	80–90	90–100
16 min.	16 min.	16 min.	16 min.	16 min.	16 min.	16 min.	16 min.	16 min.	16 min.

The third step is to write the essay after completing the multiple-choice questions. You may be able to use terms and activities that you have just seen in the multiple-choice section. The time management plan gives you 10 minutes at the end to use to check your grammar or to guess on any remaining multiple-choice items.

Texas Master Reading Teacher Test (MRTT)

MAGIC SCORE: 80 POINTS	
Case study (300–600 words)	20 points
Multiple choice (100 items)	80 points

Source: Master Reading Teacher Preparation Manual (2002–2003).

The passing score on the MRTT is a scaled score of 240 on a 100–300 point scale. You will have five hours to get it. The magic score to keep in mind is a raw score of 80 points from a combined score on both sections. To get your magic score on the multiple-choice section alone, you need to be sure on at least sixty-five questions. This allows you to get a 15 on the written portion and still pass. Table 5.6 shows how to get it.

Spend the first 20 minutes of the test surveying the data and outlining the case. More than likely, you will be looking for strengths and needs to develop a case as seen in Chapter 3.

For the multiple-choice section, plan on spending no more than 130 minutes. Use "Divide and Conquer" to divide the test into ten sections. Plan on spending no more than 13 minutes per section. Find the "gimmies" within each section and move on. Go back and

TABLE 5.6   Best Approach to MRTT

FIRST	SECOND	THIRD	LAST
Survey the data. Outline the case.	Do multiple choice.	Finish case study utilizing information from the multiple-choice items if possible.	Do remaining multiple choice.
20 min.	130 min.	130 min.	20 min.

finish any questions that you can answer with some more time, but leave the "time wasters" until the very end. Table 5.7 is a guide for how to divide your time on the multiple-choice section of the test.

TABLE 5.7   Dividing Time on Multiple Choice

1–10	10–20	20–30	30–40	40–50	50–60	60–70	70–80
13 min.	13 min.	13 min.	13 min.	13 min.	13 min.	13 min.	13 min.

After you complete as many of the multiple-choice items as you can, finish writing the case. It may be possible to use terms and activities from the examples and items from the multiple-choice questions in your writing. Finally, remember that you must obtain a 3 or better on the rubric scale for the case in order to pass. Be sure to save enough time at the end to return to the multiple choice and guess on any remaining multiple-choice items if you must do so.

Oklahoma Professional Teaching Examination (OPTE) and Oklahoma Subject Area Test (OSAT)

MAGIC SCORE: 80 POINTS	
Written portion	**30 points**
Critical analysis (150 words)	10 points
Student inquiry (150 words)	10 points
Teacher assignment (150 words)	10 points
Multiple choice (Up to 75 items)	**60 points**

Source: OSAT Study Guide, Vol. 1 (2001).

The passing score on the OPTE is 240 on a 100–300 point scale. You have four hours to get it. The magic score for the exam is likely to be an 80, where you have to obtain at least a 20 on the written portion and nail a minimum of 60 on the multiple-choice section. Table 5.8 shows the best approach to this exam.

The first step toward obtaining your magic score is to outline the essays. Be sure to review Chapter 3 carefully so that you are familiar with the forms that are most likely to appear on the exam. Then, do the multiple-choice questions for no more than two hours.

TABLE 5.8 Best Approach to OPTE and OSAT

FIRST	SECOND	THIRD	LAST
Survey the data.	Do multiple-choice questions.	Write the essays.	Do remaining multiple choice.
Outline the essays.	Pull terms and ideas from multiple choice for the essays if possible.	Spend 30 minutes per essay.	
10 min.	120 min.	90 min.	20 min.

Use the information in Chapter 3 to accomplish this. Table 5.9 is a guide for how to divide your time on the multiple-choice portion of the test.

TABLE 5.9 Dividing Time on Multiple Choice

1–10	10–20	20–30	30–40	40–50	50–60	60–70	70–75
13 min.	13 min.	13 min.	13 min.	13 min.	13 min.	13 min.	13 min.

You may have to adjust the time in this model since the multiple-choice items may be up to 75 questions. If that is the case, adjust the amount of time that you spend survey-ing the essays at the beginning and modify the amount of time that you spend at the end guessing on multiple-choice items that you could not get.

The third step in this process is to answer the short-answer questions. It may be pos-sible for you to use terms and activities pulled from the multiple-choice questions to do so. There is no particular order in which the items ought to be completed since they appear to value the same number of points. However, you probably want to answer the question that comes to you easiest, rather than wasting valuable time trying to formulate a response to a question that you are never going to get. Also, be sure to save enough time at the end to return to the multiple choice and guess on any remaining multiple-choice items.

Massachusetts Tests for Educator Licensure (MTEL–Reading)

MAGIC SCORE: 80 POINTS	
Written portion	**30 points**
Essay 1 (50–150 words)	15 points
Essay 2 (150–300 words)	15 points
Multiple choice (80 items)	**70 points**

Source: MTEL 2002–2003 Registration Bulletin.

The magic score on the MTEL is likely to be 80. Nailing the written questions on this exam allows you to go into the multiple choice with fewer burdens. The multiple-choice section has eighty questions, but remember that only seventy may count. Table 5.10 shows the best approach to this four-hour exam.

TABLE 5.10   Best Approach to MTEL–Reading

FIRST	SECOND	THIRD
Survey the data. Outline the essays.	Do multiple-choice questions. Spend 20 minutes per section.	Finish the essays and use terms and ideas from multiple choice if possible. Spend 25 minutes per essay.
10 min.	160 min.	50 min.

First, you should survey the essays. You may receive two essay questions that look similar to the short answers in Chapter 3, or you may receive one case study question and either a procedural, justification, or lesson plan question. If you receive a case study, you are going to need more time. Adjust the time by shortening the amount of time that you spend on the multiple-choice items from 160 minutes to 120 minutes. Table 5.11 reflects the amount of time to spend on the multiple-choice items if you have 160 minutes. If you end up shortening the time to 120 minutes, use the distributions shown in Table 5.12.

TABLE 5.11   Dividing Time on Multiple Choice (160 Minutes)

1–10	10–20	20–30	30–40	40–50	50–60	60–70	70–80
20 min.	20 min.	20 min.	20 min.	20 min.	20 min.	20 min.	20 min.

TABLE 5.12   Dividing Time on Multiple Choice (120 Minutes)

1–10	10–20	20–30	30–40	40–50	50–60	60–70	70–80
13 min.	13 min.	13 min.	13 min.	13 min.	13 min.	13 min.	13 min.

After you complete as many multiple-choice items as you can answer easily, return to the short-answer questions. You may be able to use terms and activities from the multiple-choice questions. If both short-answer questions value the same number of points, do the one that comes easiest to you. There is no sense in wasting time on a question that you cannot answer. However, if one question is worth more points than the other, do the question that earns you the most points first. You move closer to your magic score that way. Be sure to save enough time at the end to return to the multiple choice and guess on any remaining multiple-choice items if you must do so.

Colorado Program for Licensing Assessments for Colorado Educators (PLACE)

MAGIC SCORE: 80 POINTS	
Written portion	**20 points**
Essay (300 words)	20 points
Multiple-choice (80–100 items)	**80 points**

Source: PLACE Study Guide, Vol. 2 (2001).

A passing score on the Colorado PLACE is 220 on a 100–300 point scale. You have four and one-half hours to get it. Each assessment includes a written response and multiple-choice section. Be sure to read Chapter 3 carefully because it provides you with information on answering essay questions. The multiple choice has approximately eighty scored questions. To reach the magic score of 80, you should prepare to do really well on the written portion or exceptionally well on the multiple-choice items. The written section is easier to control, so if you earn 15 points there and at least 65 on the multiple-choice section, a passing score is well within grasp. Table 5.13 shows the best approach to the exam.

TABLE 5.13 Best Approach to Colorado PLACE

FIRST	SECOND	THIRD
Survey the data.	Do the multiple choice for 160 minutes.	Write the essay.
Outline the essay.	Pull terms and ideas for essays if possible.	
10 min.	160 min.	100 min.

First, survey the data and outline the essay. Then, do the multiple choice for no more than 160 minutes. Try to nail the "gimmies" and work on the items that you can get with a little extra effort. Skip the ones that you know that you will never get. Table 5.14 shows you a way to divide your time effectively.

TABLE 5.14 Dividing Time on Multiple Choice

1–10	10–20	20–30	30–40	40–50	50–60	60–70	70–80
20 min.	20 min.	20 min.	20 min.	20 min.	20 min.	20 min.	20 min.

The third step in this process is to write the essay. You may be able to use terms and activities that you have just seen in the multiple-choice section. Be sure to save enough time at the end to return to the multiple choice and guess on any remaining multiple-choice items.

New York State Teacher Certification
Exam/Assessment of Teaching Skills
(NYSTCE/ATS–Written)

MAGIC SCORE: 80 POINTS	
Written portion	**20 points**
Essay (300 words)	20 points
Multiple choice (80 items)	**80 points**

Source: NYSTCE Assessment of Teaching Skills—Written Preparation Guide (2000).

A passing score on the ATS–Written exam is 220. You have four hours to get it. The format includes both a written response and multiple-choice section. The multiple-choice section contains eighty questions, though an unnamed number of them do not count. The estimated magic score on the test is 80. The points that you need to pass are estimated to be a minimum of 15 on the written portion and a minimum of 65 on the multiple choice. The best approach to the exam is shown in Table 5.15.

TABLE 5.15   Best Approach to NYSTCE/ATS–Written

FIRST	SECOND	THIRD
Survey the data.	Do the multiple-choice section.	Complete the essay after the multiple-choice section using terms and ideas from it if possible.
Outline the short answer.	Spend no more than 15 minutes per section.	
10 min.	120 min.	100 min.

First, survey the data for the essay and supply an outline for it. Then, move on to the multiple choice section. Plan on spending no more than 15 minutes per section. Table 5.16 serves as a guide.

TABLE 5.16   Dividing Time on Multiple Choice

1–10	10–20	20–30	30–40	40–50	50–60	60–70	70–80
15 min.	15 min.	15 min.	15 min.	15 min.	15 min.	15 min.	15 min.

After completing the multiple-choice section, turn to the essay and write it. You may be able to import terms and activities from the multiple-choice section that help you in this endeavor. Any remaining time should be spent on guessing on multiple-choice items that you could not complete.

Texas Examinations of Educator Standards (TExES)

MAGIC SCORE: 80 POINTS	
Multiple choice (125 items)	100 points

Source: Texas Examinations of Educator Standards, http://www.texes.nesinc.com.

The TExES is a five-hour exam with a passing score of 240 on a 100–300 point scale. There are 125 items, but only 100 are scored. The magic score on this test is approximately 80. This means that you have to make good attempts on a minimum of 90 items. Table 5.17 shows how to get that magic score.

TABLE 5.17 Dividing Time on Multiple Choice

1–15	15–30	30–45	45–60	60–75	75–90	90–105	105–120	120–125	REMAINING ITEMS
30 min.	30 min.	30 min.	30 min.	30 min.	30 min.	30 min.	30 min.	30 min.	30 min.

You must work the test in sections. Spend no more than thirty minutes per section. Your goal is to identify the "gimmies" in each section, along with the questions that you can answer with a little more time and effort. Remember that you are going to encounter questions that are true "time wasters" and items that are not even going to count toward your passing score. You must be very methodical in your approach.

Texas Examination for the Certification of Educators in Texas (ExCET)

MAGIC SCORE: 80 POINTS	
Multiple choice (125 questions)	100 points

Source: Texas Examinations of Educator Standards, http://www.excet.nesinc.com.

The ExCET is a five-hour exam with a passing score of 70 on a 0–100 point scale. There are 125 items, but only 100 are scored. The magic score on this test is approximately 80. This means that you have to make good attempts on a minimum of ninety items. Table 5.18 shows how to get that magic score.

TABLE 5.18 Dividing Time on Multiple Choice

1–15	15–30	30–45	45–60	60–75	75–90	90–105	105–120	120–125	REMAINING ITEMS
30 min.	30 min.	30 min.	30 min.	30 min.	30 min.	30 min.	30 min.	30 min.	30 min.

You must work the test in sections. Spend no more than thirty minutes per section. Your goal is to identify the "gimmies" in each section, along with the questions that you can answer with a little more time and effort. Remember that you are going to encounter questions that are true "time wasters" and items that are not even going to count toward your passing score. You must be very methodical in your approach.

Michigan Test for Teacher Certification (MTTC)

MAGIC SCORE: 75 POINTS	
Multiple choice (100 items)	80 points

Source: MTTC Study Guide, Vol. 2 (2001).

The MTTC is a four and one-half hour exam with a passing score of 220 on a 100–300 point scale. The exam includes one hundred multiple-choice items, but only eighty items are scored. To obtain this score, you need a magic score of 80 and need to methodically answer ninety questions. Table 5.19 shows how to get it.

TABLE 5.19   Dividing Time on Multiple Choice

1–15	15–30	30–45	45–60	60–75	75–90	90–100	REMAINING ITEMS
40 min.	40 min.	40 min.	40 min.	40 min.	40 min.	20 min.	10 min.

You must work the test in sections. Spend no more than forty minutes per section. Your goal is to identify the "gimmies" in each section, along with the questions that you can answer with a little more time and effort. Remember that you are going to encounter questions that are true "time wasters" and items that are not even going to count toward your passing score. You must be very methodical in your approach.

Illinois Certification Testing System (ICTS)

MAGIC SCORE: 80 POINTS	
Multiple choice (125 items)	100 points

Source: ICTS Study Guide (1996).

The ICTS is a five-hour exam with a passing score of 70 on a 0–100 point scale. The exam includes 125 multiple-choice items, but only one hundred items are scored. To obtain this score, you need to be sure of your answers on at least ninety items to approach the magic score of 80. Table 5.20 shows how to get that magic score.

TABLE 5.20   Dividing Time on Multiple Choice

1–15	15–30	30–45	45–60	60–75	75–90	90–105	105–120	120–125	REMAINING ITEMS
30 min.	30 min.	30 min.	30 min.	30 min.	30 min.	30 min.	30 min.	30 min.	30 min.

You must work the test in sections. Spend no more than thirty minutes per section. Your goal is to identify the "gimmies" in each section, along with the questions that you can answer with a little more time and effort. Remember that you are going to encounter questions that are true "time wasters" and items that are not even going to count toward your passing score. You must be very methodical in your approach.

CONCLUSION

What you have learned throughout this chapter are ways to handle both written and multiple-choice tests or multiple-choice-only exams, strategies to manage your time, and the best approaches for reaching your magic score. Be sure to verify the formats and the point distributions described in Chapter 1 since these tests can change without notice (adjust your strategies accordingly if that becomes the case). Information about changes is also posted at http://www.ablongman.com/boosalis as it becomes available.

The final chapter of this book presents a study plan that you can adapt to your schedule. The study plan shows you how to learn the content of Chapter 2 effectively, along with the standards for your state and the data analysis methods that you must know for the test. You are encouraged to answer all of the questions posed in Chapter 6, which use the formats described in Chapter 3, regardless of whether your exam has essays. This way, you can rest assured that you have studied as completely as possible the content of Chapter 2 as it relates to the major reading instruction model.

CHAPTER SIX

THE MAGIC PLAN

This chapter presents a four-week study plan and is an important one for you to complete. One essential ingredient in your studies is the official multiple-choice and practice essays that the test company may provide. We recommend avoiding contrived multiple-choice items from sources other than from the company that develops your test since phony questions may not align with the exam at all.

Many official materials are also available online. Your state department of education's Web page has information on the testing programs and may post the official guides that you can download. Visit http://www.ablongman.com/boosalis for the direct link to your state's education department. Restrictions may apply to who is permitted to view these materials, so read the site information very carefully. Study guides can also be ordered directly from the company. The registration bulletins should provide that information to you, and the price is generally under $10 per copy. Some restrictions may apply to who can order these guides, but it is worth the effort and expense to locate and purchase them.

A FOUR-WEEK PLAN

Table 6.1 shows the four-week plan. Read it over carefully first and then develop your own study schedule if your time does not permit strict adherence to the plan.

TABLE 6.1   Four-Week Plan

WEEK 1					
What to Read					
MONDAY	**TUESDAY**	**WEDNESDAY**	**THURSDAY**	**FRIDAY**	**WEEKEND**
Chapter 1 Chapter 6	Chapter 2	Chapter 2	Chapter 2	Chapters 3 and 4	Review

TABLE 6.1   CONTINUED

General Questions

- What is a magic score?
- What is the magic score for your test?
- How do you obtain it for your exam?

WEEK 2

Monday–Tuesday

1. Complete tables from Appendix A (assessment to spelling).
2. Complete table from Appendix B for your state's standards from assessment to spelling.
3. Read Chapter 3.

Wednesday–Friday   Chapter 2

1. Complete tables from Appendix A (vocabulary to written language).
2. Complete table from Appendix B for your state's standards from fluency to written language.
3. Read Chapter 4.

WEEK 3

Study Questions for Monday

- How do individual assessments differ from group (standardized) assessments?
- How do norm-referenced assessments differ from criterion-referenced tests?
- Write a brief procedural essay on administering an informal reading inventory to determine a student's independent reading level.
- Imagine that a first-grade teacher uses a miscue analysis to analyze a student's oral reading errors. She analyzes the student's use of graphophonic, syntactic, and semantic cues when making the errors. Using your knowledge of miscue analyses, write a response in which you justify one way that the analysis can inform your knowledge of the student's ability to read independently.
- Write a brief procedural essay on administering a running record.
- Write a brief procedural essay for communicating the results of both norm-referenced and criterion-referenced tests to parents (any grade level).

Study Questions for Tuesday

Concepts about Print

- Write a procedural essay that describes the steps for assessing concepts about print.
- Write a procedural essay that describes the steps for conducting a concepts-about-print activity in a kindergarten classroom.
- Write a procedural essay that describes the steps for instructing students in learning the letters of the alphabet.

Phonemic Awareness

- Write a procedural essay for assessing a kindergarten student's level of phonemic awareness.
- A kindergarten teacher uses an activity that asks students to sort pictures of common words (for example, *cars, kites, cats*) into groups by initial sound. Using your knowledge of phonemic

(continued)

TABLE 6.1   CONTINUED

awareness, write a response in which you justify a way that this activity can help to develop the students' literacy development.

■ Write a procedural essay for teaching students how to segment spoken words into individual phonemes (use Elkonin sound boxes).

Phonics

■ Write a procedural essay for assessing phonics skills of children.
■ Write a procedural essay for teaching students to make words using simple onsets and rimes (see Chapter 3, Writing Lesson Plans for Decoding).
■ A kindergarten teacher distributes letters to children and has them assemble a common rime (for example, *-at*). She then has the children create words using the rime by placing common consonants in front of the rime and reading the words aloud. Using your knowledge of phonics instruction, write an essay in which you justify one way that the activity can enhance the students' reading development.
■ Write a procedural essay for teaching students high-frequency words (see Chapter 2, Level 2: Decoding (Kindergarten through Third Grade).

Spelling

■ Write a procedural essay for teaching students to move from the pre-phonetic to the phonetic stage of spelling.
■ Write a procedural essay for teaching students to move from the phonetic to the transitional stage of spelling.
■ Write a procedural essay for teaching students to spell high-frequency words.

Study Questions for Wednesday

Fluency

■ Describe a procedure for assessing fluency and accuracy.
■ Describe a procedure for using choral reading to build fluency and expression
■ Describe a procedure for using predictable text to build fluency.

Study Questions for Thursday

■ A fifth-grade teacher uses syllabication to teach students to divide unknown words into syllables. She then teaches them to analyze each part of the word structurally for meaningful parts before the words are reassembled and pronounced. Using your knowledge of syllabication and structural analysis, write an essay in which you justify one way that the activity described above can help the students understand polysyllabic, content-area words.
■ Describe a procedure for teaching students to understand the meanings of vocabulary words by structurally analyzing them for prefixes and suffixes.
■ A fourth-grade teacher uses context clues to teach her students to preteach the meanings of several difficult vocabulary words. Using your knowledge of vocabulary development, write an essay in which you justify one way that the activity described above can enhance these students' knowledge of vocabulary words.

TABLE 6.1 CONTINUED

Comprehension

- Describe a procedure for teaching students to understand the relationship between questions they are asked and answers they must provide (use QAR).
- A fifth-grade teacher presents the following words to her students: *good, bad, terrible, wonderful, awful*. Working in pairs, students then rate a list of experiences (for example, eating chocolate cake, babysitting a brother or sister, doing homework) using these terms. She then conducts a whole-class discussion about how each pair rated the experiences. Using your knowledge of teaching fact and opinion, write an essay that justifies one way that this activity can enhance the students' reading development.
- Describe a procedure for using KWL for teaching students pre-, while-, and post-reading activities.

Narrative Text

- Describe a procedure for teaching students to respond to literature (use reading logs).
- Describe an activity to teach students to comprehend narrative text literally and inferentially.

Content-Area Literacy

- Describe a procedure for teaching students expository text structure.
- Describe a procedure for teaching students to retrieve and retain information from expository text (use SQ3R).

Independent and At-home Reading

- A fourth-grade student who reads grade-level texts fluently and accurately comments that he really doesn't like to read. Using your knowledge of motivating students to read, describe a procedure appropriate for accomplishing this goal.
- Recently, caregivers of children in a third-grade class have asked the teacher for ways that they can get involved in their children's reading at home. The teacher develops a plan that has the students take their independent-level books home with them to read each night to the caregivers. The teacher also develops a general list of high-level interest books appropriate for children at that grade level that caregivers can obtain at their local library to read with their children. She even includes a list of simple activities that they can perform with their children as they read to their children each night for half an hour (for example, modeling concepts about print, intonation, etc.). Using your knowledge of "parental" involvement in literacy, describe one way that the activities described above can help to develop the children's literacy skills.

Study Questions for Friday

- A fourth-grade teacher wishes to incorporate discussion groups in her reading classroom. Describe a procedure for accomplishing this goal.
- A sixth-grade teacher wishes to incorporate the language experience approach in his classroom. Describe a procedure for accomplishing this goal.

(continued)

TABLE 6.1   CONTINUED

- An eighth-grade teacher wishes to use the process approach to writing on a unit that she is planning on the environment. Describe a procedure for accomplishing this goal.
- Write a brief procedural essay for arranging centers in your classroom.
- Write a brief procedural essay for selecting texts in both kindergarten through third grade and fourth through eighth grade.
- A first-grade teacher groups children together by need. In one group, the teacher works directly with children who have difficulty visually discriminating similar letters (for example, *b* and *p*), while another group of students sits together and choral-reads a story with the teacher's aide. Using your knowledge of homogeneous grouping, write a brief essay that justifies the way that the teacher has arranged these students in his classroom.
- Use the model unit plan to create thematic or interdisciplinary unit.

WEEK 4

This week is the prelude to your success. Review the completed tables from Appendix A and B and the essays from your notebook simultaneously. You may simply read them to yourself or write them out a few times until they come naturally. The purpose of this activity is to ensure that you have the tables in mind when analyzing data and answering multiple-choice questions. A sample data set for decoding, comprehension, and a case study appears in Appendix C to help you to sharpen your data analysis and writing skills. If you need to do so, reread Chapters 3 and 4 to refresh your memory on data analysis.

You should have received your study guides or downloaded them by now. They are essential in your study. Apply all of the strategies discussed, from how to obtain your magic score (Chapter 1) to the strategies for writing essays (Chapter 3) and completing multiple choice (Chapter 4). Be sure to replicate the conditions of the test as closely as possible. Practice timing yourself and get into the habit of either checking your watch frequently or placing your watch at the head of the desk or table to keep track of your time. Ideally, you will give yourself three attempts at the exams that you have received, so that you will not be surprised on test day. Spend your last week practicing the multiple choice items, rewriting essays, and reviewing standards.

Test Day

In addition to the obvious considerations of getting enough nourishment and sleep prior to test day, there are several reminders to end this chapter with.

1. *Know your magic score.* Know what score you are aiming for on the test. Review Chapter 1 and contact the test representative in your state to confirm as much of the information as you can before testing.
2. *Know how to obtain your magic score.* Understand the procedures to manage time overall on your test. Time can be a great hindrance to a successful performance, so be sure that you know how to manage your time before test day.
3. *Use written and multiple-choice strategies.* Know the strategies for the written and multiple-choice sections, and make sure that you have had the chance to practice them on the study guides that you have obtained.
4. *Visit http://www.ablongman.com/boosalis for any new information about your exam.*
5. *Dress comfortably and bring earplugs.* Since you can neither control the location of the exam nor its environment, be sure to dress for test success. That means wearing comfortable clothes. A layer or two is a good idea, depending on the season, since you can more easily re-

TABLE 6.1 CONTINUED

move a sweater than ask the test proctor to turn the thermostat either up or down. Foam ear-plugs are another good idea. They can be purchased at your local pharmacy. One candidate reported that the person next to her sighed constantly during the exam—not loudly, but audibly enough to be a distraction to this particular candidate—and it ruined her experience. So it may be a good idea for you to use earplugs during the exam. Try them out prior to test day. Follow the directions that accompany the package for use.

6. *Be confident!* If you have studied the content, practiced the study guides, learned the standards, and written all of the essays, you are in an excellent position to do your best on the exam. Unless others have used this book in their preparation, probably no one in the room knows as much about your exam or the core model of reading instruction like you do. Take pride in that—and beat the exam!

STUDY FRAMES FOR CHAPTER 2

OVERVIEW OF DECODING INSTRUCTION			
(First)		**(Second)** **Explicit Decoding Instruction**	**(Third)** **Ultimate Aim**
Concepts about Print		Sight Words	

PHONEMIC AWARENESS			
			Segmenting Spoken Words
ACTIVITIES			

CONCEPTS ABOUT PRINT				
	Print Carries Meaning		Words in Sentences	

EXPLICIT DECODING AREAS				
		Phonics Generalizations		Polysyllabic Word Decoding
ACTIVITIES				

SPELLING DEVELOPMENT			
	Phonetic		Conventional
■ ■ Encoding specific sounds	■ ■ Encoding medial vowels ■	■ ■ Writing by letter pattern	■ ■ Complex word families
(example)	(example)	(example)	(example)

FLUENCY			
Teacher-Directed Reading		Independent/At-Home Reading	
			At-Home Reading

COMPONENTS OF READING COMPREHENSION		
Fluency	Vocabulary Development	Comprehension Levels

VOCABULARY FOR COMPREHENSION			
Morphology for Structural Analysis		Word Types	Context
Inflectional Suffixes	Roots and Derivations		

VOCABULARY ACTIVITIES		
Vocabulary Development	Structural Analysis	Using Context
Elaboration Activities	*Roots and*	

READING COMPREHENSION		
Literal Comprehension		
Memory Questions	Interpretation Questions	Higher-Order Questions

STRATEGIES FOR COMPREHENSION		
	While-Reading	
Prereading Strategies		Elaboration Strategies

ORAL AND WRITTEN LANGUAGE DEVELOPMENT				
		Written Language Activities		
Strategy Discussions		Emergent		

LEVEL 2: DECODING (KINDERGARTEN THROUGH THIRD GRADE)				
Concepts about Print			Sight Words	

LEVEL 3: FLUENCY	

			Schema Strategies
LEVEL 4: READING COMPREHENSION (THIRD GRADE THROUGH EIGHTH GRADE)			

STANDARD TABLES

*Please list your state's standards for each area of the model from Chapter 2. Try to learn both the content of Chapter 2 and the standards together as you study.

AREA	K	1	2	3	4	5	6	7 +
Concepts about Print								
Phonemic Awareness								
Decoding and Spelling								
Fluency								
Vocabulary								
Comprehension *Literal* *Inferential* *Evaluative*								
Narrative Text								
Expository Text								

Study Skills	**Independent and at-home reading**	**Oral Language Skills**	**Written Language** *Syntax* *Forms* *Styles*	**At-Risk Children**

■ ■ ■ ■ ■

DATA SETS FOR LESSON PLAN
AND CASE STUDY LESSON PLAN
FOR DECODING

Data Set for Decoding

SPELLING ITEMS	CHILD'S SPELLING
cat	kt
rat	rt
hat	ht
mat	mt
sat	st

A Possible Decoding-Related Question

Based on your analysis of the spelling data, write an essay that demonstrates the following. First, state the need reflected in the data. Second, describe instruction to remedy the need you have identified. Third, state the benefit of the instruction you described.

Decoding Question Frame

FORM	CONTENT
■ Need	
■ Scaffolding Lesson Plan	Strategy:

■ Scaffolding   Materials:
Lesson Plan
(continued)

Steps:

■ Benefit

LESSON PLAN FOR COMPREHENSION

A Possible Lesson Plan for Comprehension Question

Did you know that the ocean stays warm long into the night? You might think that it is because the sun shines on it all day, which makes it hot. But even on cool and cloudy days, the ocean's temperature can still be warm after dark. How can that be?

The reason is that the sun's light is made up of waves. The waves are neither hot nor cold. The light waves penetrate the surface of the ocean and charge it, much like a battery. At night, the ocean releases all of the energy that it has been storing all day long. That's what makes the water feel warm at night.

Teacher: Can you tell me what you were reading about?

Student: It's about the ocean.

Teacher: What does it say about the ocean?

Student: It says that it stays hot long into the night.

Teacher: Does it tell you why it stays hot all night?

Student: Yes. It says that the sun shines on it all day and that it heats up the water.

Teacher: Can you read this part for me? (Points to third sentence of second paragraph)

Student: "The light waves penetrate the surface of the ocean and charge it, much like a battery." Oh, maybe it is something else that makes the ocean stay warm at night.

Question

Based on your analysis of the teacher and student conversation, write an essay that demonstrates the following. First, state the need reflected in the data. Second, describe instruction to remedy the need you have identified. Third, state the benefit of the instruction you described.

Comprehension Question Frame

FORM	CONTENT

■ Need

■ Scaffolding
Lesson Plan

■ Benefit

A POSSIBLE CASE STUDY QUESTION

QUESTION

This case study focuses on a student named Chris. The data sets below describe his reading performance during the early part of third grade. Using this data set, write a response in which you apply your knowledge of literacy development to this case. Your response should include three parts:

Item 1: State three strengths and needs reflected in the data.

Item 2: Write two leson plans for this student.

Item 3: Explain how these lesson plans will help the student's development.

Super Bowl Sunday was a day that Bob had been waiting for. It took forever for the day to arrive, and Bob looked forward to watching his favorite team, the Bulldogs, play the most important game of the season.

For weeks, he had cheered his team on. With his mother's help, he even called a radio program to offer the team support. Now, finally, the day arrived. His family even told him that it was his day the night before.

"Bob," his mother called, "I need to talk to you." Bob approached his mother. "Your cousin Martin is coming," she said. "His mother is very sick and we need to look after him for a couple of days."

Bob was indignant but said nothing. He knew that Martin had a disability and that he would scream louder than even Bob could if he didn't get his way—he also knew that Martin couldn't help it. Martin's favorite program was *Star Trek,* and it was on at the worst possible time.

TEACHER/STUDENT DIALOGUE

Teacher: Tell me what you were reading about.

Chris: It's a story about a boy named Bob who's going to watch the Super Bowl.

Teacher: What else can you tell me?

Chris: The name of the team is the Bulldogs. Oh, and his cousin Martin is coming.

Teacher: What can you tell me about Martin?

Chris: He likes *Star Trek.*

Teacher: Is there anything special about Martin?

Chris: Yes. He can scream louder than Bob can.

Teacher: How does Bob feel about Martin coming over?

Chris: Happy, because they get to watch the game together.

WRITING SUMMARY

This is a story about Bob. Bob likes football. He is going to watch the Super Bowl with his cousin, Martin. Martin is coming over because his mother is very sick. They are going to watch the game and have fun, because Martin can scream louder than Bob can.

ASSESSMENT AREA	BOB'S SCORES	GOAL
1. Decoding	Third Grade	Third Grade
2. Spelling	6	5
3. Main ideas	4	5
4. Inferences	1	4
5. Polysyllabic words	3	5
6. Prefix/root/suffixes	1	5

Case Study Frame

FORM	CONTENT
Strength 1	
Strength 2	
Problem	
Need A	
Need B	
Need A	
Lesson Plan	
Benefit	
Need B	
Lesson Plan	
Benefit	

BIBLIOGRAPHY

Adams, M. J. (1990). *Beginning to read: Thinking and learning about print.* Cambridge, MA: MIT Press.

Adams, M. J., & Bruck, M. (1995, Summer). Resolving the "great debate." *American Educator, 19,* 7, 10–20.

AEPA Registration Bulletin (2002). NES Inc. & Arizona Dept. of Ed.

Adamson, H. D. (1993). *Academic competence—Theory and classroom practice: Preparing ESL students for content courses.* New York: Longman.

Alexandrowicz, V. (2002). Effective instruction for second language learners: What tutors must know. *Reading Improvement, 39,* 71–79.

Alvermann, D. E., & Hayes, D. A. (1989). Classroom discussion of content area reading assignments: An intervention study. *Reading Research Quarterly, 24,* 305–335.

Anderson, S. A. (2000). How parental involvement makes a difference in reading achievement. *Reading Improvement, 37,* 61–87.

Anderson, V., & Roit, M. (1993). Planning and implementing collaborative strategy instruction for delayed readers in grades 6–10. *The Elementary School Journal, 94,* 121–137.

Armbruster, B. B., Anderson, T. H., & Ostertag, J. (1987). Does text structure/summarization instruction facilitate learning from expository text? *Reading Research Quarterly, 22,* 331–346.

Armbruster, B. B., & Nagy, W. E. (1992). Vocabulary in content area lessons. *The Reading Teacher, 45,* 550–551.

Asher, J. (1982). *Learning another language through actions: The complete teachers' guidebook.* Los Gatos, CA: Sky Oaks.

Au, K. H., & Scheu, J. A. (1989). Guiding students to interpret a novel. *The Reading Teacher, 43,* 104–110.

Ausubel, D. (1963). *The psychology of meaningful verbal learning.* New York: Grune & Stratton.

Babbs, P. J., & Moe, A. J. (1983). Metacognition: A key for independent learning from text. *The Reading Teacher, 37,* 422–426.

Ball, E. W., & Blachman, B. A. (1988). Phoneme segmentation training: Effect on reading readiness. *Annals of Dyslexia, 38,* 208–224.

Ball, E. W., & Blachman, B. A. (1991). Does phoneme awareness training in kindergarten make a difference in early word recognition and developmental spelling? *Reading Research Quarterly, 26,* 49–66.

Barnitz, J. G. (1998). Revising grammar instruction for authentic composing and comprehending. *The Reading Teacher, 51,* 608–611.

Barrentine, S. (1996). Engaging with reading through interactive read alouds. *The Reading Teacher, 50,* 36–43.

Bauman, J. F., & Bergerson, B. S. (1993). Story map instruction using children's literature: Effects on first graders' comprehension of central narrative elements. *Journal of Reading Behavior, 25,* 407–438.

Bauman, J. F., & Schmitt, M. C. (1986). The what, why, how, and when of comprehension instruction. *The Reading Teacher, 40,* 640–647.

Bauman, J. F., Seifert-Kessell, N., & Jones, L. A. (1992). Effect of think aloud instruction on elementary students' comprehension monitoring ability. *Journal of Reading Behavior, 25,* 407–438.

Baxendell, B. W. (2003). Consistent, coherent, creative: The three c's of graphic organizers. *Teaching Exceptional Children, 35,* 46–55.

Bear, D. R., & Barone, D. (1989). Using children's spellings to group for word study and directed reading in the primary classroom. *Reading Psychology, 10,* 275–292.

Bear, D. R., & McIntosh, M. E. (1990). Directed reading-thinking activities: Four activities to promote thinking and study habits in social studies. *Social Education, 54,* 385–388.

Bear, D. R., & Templeton, S. (1998). Explorations in developmental spelling: Foundations for learning and teaching phonics, spelling, and vocabulary. *The Reading Teacher, 52,* 222–242.

Beck, I. L., & Juel, C. (1995, Summer). The role of decoding in learning to read. *American Educator,* 8–42.

Beiger, E. M. (1987). Making connections: Alternatives to the vocabulary notebook. *The Reading Teacher, 41,* 132–138.

Beiger, E. M. (1995/1996). Promoting multicultural education through a literature-based approach. *The Reading Teacher, 49,* 308–312.

Boosalis, C. N. (2003). Effective time-management models for the constructed response portion of the Reading Instruction Competence Assessment. *The California Reader 36,* 26–36.

Bottomley, D. M., Henk, W. A., & Melnick, S. A. (1997/1998). Assessing children's views about themselves as writers using the writer self-perception scale. *The Reading Teacher, 51,* 286–296.

Bryan, J. (1998). KWWL: Questioning the known. *The Reading Teacher, 51,* 618–624.

Burns, P. C., Roe, B. D., & Ross, E. P. (1999). *Teaching reading in today's elementary schools.* Boston: Houghton Mifflin.

Button, K., Johnson, M. J., & Furgerson, P. (1996). Interactive writing in a primary classroom. *The Reading Teacher, 49,* 446–454.

Carr, E. M., & Mazur-Stewart, M. (1988). The effects of vocabulary instruction overview guides on vocabulary comprehension and retention. *Journal of Reading Behavior, 20,* 43–62.

Carr, K. S. (1983). The importance of inference skills in the primary grades. *The Reading Teacher, 36,* 518–522.

Carr, K. S., Dewitz, P., & Patberg, J. (1989). Using cloze for inference training. *The Reading Teacher, 42,* 380–385.

Carr, K. S., & Ogle, D. (1987). KWL plus: A strategy for comprehension and summarization. *Journal of Reading, 30,* 626–631.

Caverly, D. C., Mandeville, T. F., & Nicholson, S. A. (1995). Plan: A study-reading strategy for informational text. *Journal of Adolescent & Adult Literacy, 39,* 190–199.

Chall, J. (1996). *Stages of reading development.* Fort Worth, TX: Harcourt Brace.

Chamot, A., & O'Malley, J. (1994). *The CALLA handbook: Implementing the cognitive academic language learning approach.* Reading, PA: Addison Wesley.

Chan, L. K. (1996). Motivational orientations and metacognitive abilities of intellectually gifted children. *Gifted Child Quarterly, 40,* 184–193.

Chard, D., & Dickson, S. V. (1999). Phonological awareness: Instructional and assessment guidelines. *Intervention in Schools and Clinic, 34,* 261–270.

Chase, A. C., & Duffelmeyer, F. A. (1990). Vocab-lit: Integrating vocabulary study and literature study. *Journal of Reading, 34,* 188–193.

Cioffi, G. (1992). Perspective and experience: Developing critical reading abilities. *Journal of Reading, 36,* 48–52.

Clay, M. M. (1993a). *An observation survey of early literacy achievement.* Portsmouth, NH: Heinemann.

Clay, M. M. (1993b). *Reading recovery: A guidebook for teachers.* Portsmouth, NH: Heinemann.

Commander, N. E., & Smith, B. D. (1996). Learning logs: A tool for cognitive monitoring. *Journal of Adolescent and Adult Literacy, 36,* 446–453.

Cooper, J. D., & Kiger, N. D. (2003). *Literacy: Helping children construct meaning,* 5th ed. Boston: Houghton Mifflin.

Courtney, A. M., & Abodeeb, T. L. (1999). Diagnostic-reflective portfolios. *The Reading Teacher, 52,* 708–714.

CSET. (2002–2003a). *Registration Bulletin.* California Commission on Teacher Credentialing and National Evaluation Systems, Inc.

CSET. (2002–2003b). *Registration Bulletin* [and test information]. Retrieved February 2, 2003; from http://www.cset.nesinc.com

Cunningham, P. M. (1978). Decoding polysyllabic words: An alternative strategy. *Journal of Reading, 21,* 608–614.

Cunningham, P. M. (1980). Applying a compare/contrast process to identifying polysyllabic words. *Journal of Reading Behavior, 12,* 213–223.

Davey, B. (1983). Think aloud—Modeling the cognitive processes of reading comprehension. *Journal of Reading, 27,* 44–47.

DiCecco, U. M., & Gleason, M. M. (2002). Using graphic organizers to attain relational knowledge from expository text. *Teaching Exceptional Children, 35,* 306–320.

DiStephano, P. P., & Hagerty, P. J. (1985). Teaching spelling at the elementary level: A realistic perspective. *The Reading Teacher, 38,* 372–377.

Dowhower, S. L. (1999). Supporting a strategic stance in the classroom: A comprehension framework for helping teachers help students to be strategic. *The Reading Teacher, 52,* 672–688.

Duffelmeyer, F. A. (1994). Effective anticipation guide statements for learning from expository text. *Journal of Reading, 37,* 452–457.

Duffelmeyer, F. A., & Baum, D. D. (1992). The extended anticipation guide. *Journal of Reading, 35,* 654–656.

Dunn, A. H., & Graves, M. F. (1987). Intensive vocabulary instruction as a prewriting technique. *Reading Research Quarterly, 22,* 311–329.

Ediger, M. (1999). Evaluation of reading progress. *Reading Improvement, 36,* 50–56.

Erhi, L. C., Nunes, S. R., Stahl, S. A., & Willows, D. M. (2001). Systematic phonics instruction helps students learn to read: Evidence from the National Reading Panel's meta-analysis. *Review of Educational Research, 71,* 393–447.

Erhi, L. C., Nunes, S. R., Willows, D. M., Schuster, B. V., Yaghuoub-Zadeh, Z., & Shannahan, T. (2002). Phonemic awareness instruction helps children learn to read: Evidence from the National Reading Panel's meta-analysis. *Reading Research Quarterly, 36,* 250–287.

Farr, R., & Tone, B. (1998). *Portfolio and performance assessment: Helping students evaluate their progress as readers and writers,* 2nd ed. Orlando, FL: Harcourt Brace.

Fielding, L. G., & Pearson, D. (1994). Reading comprehension: What works. *Educational Leadership, 51,* 62–68.

Fitzgerald, J. (1993). Literacy and students who are learning English as a second language. *The Reading Teacher, 46,* 638–647.

Fitzgerald, J., & Spiegel, D. L. (1983). Enhancing children's reading comprehension through instruction in narrative text structure. *Journal of Reading Behavior, 15,* 1–17.

Fowler, G. L. (1982). Developing comprehension skills in primary grades through the use of story frames. *The Reading Teacher, 35,* 176–179.

Gagne, E. (1985). *The cognitive psychology of school learning.* Boston: Little, Brown.

Gambrell, L. B. (1985). Dialogue journals: Reading-writing interaction. *The Reading Teacher, 35,* 512–515.

Garner, R., & Gillingham, M. G. (1987). Students' knowledge of text structure. *Journal of Reading Behavior, 19,* 247–259.

Gass, S. M., & Selinker, L. (1994). *Second language acquisition: An introductory course.* Hillsdale, NJ: Lawrence Erlbaum Associates.

Gersten, R., Fuchs, L. S., Williams, J. P., & Baker, S. (2001). Teaching reading comprehension strategies to students with learning disabilities: A review of the research. *Review of Educational Research, 71,* 279–320.

Gifford, A. P. (2000). Broadening concepts through vocabulary development. *Reading Improvement, 37,* 2–11.

Goodman, K. (1996). *On reading: A common-sense look at the nature of language and the science of reading.* Portsmouth, NH: Heinemann.

Gray-Schlegel, M. A., & King, Y. (1998). Introducing concepts about print to the preservice teacher: A hands-on experience. *The California Reader, 32,* 16–21.

Griffith, P. L., & Olson, M. W. (1992). Phonemic awareness helps readers break the code. *The Reading Teacher, 45,* 516–523.

Groff, P. (1998). Groff responds to Lapp and Flood. *The Reading Teacher, 52,* 144.

Gunning, T. G. (2003). *Creating literacy instruction for all children,* 5th ed. Boston: Allyn & Bacon.

Hancock, M. R. (1992). Literature response journals: Insights beyond the printed page. *Language Arts, 69,* 36–42.

Hanson, J., & Pearson, P. D. (1983). An instructional study: Improving the inferential comprehension of good and poor fourth-grade readers. *Journal of Educational Psychology, 75,* 821–829.

Henning, D. & Pickett, A. (2000). *A study of improving sight and functional vocabulary development and comprehension.* M.A. Research Project, Saint Xavier University and SkyLight Professional Development. (Eric Document Reproduction Service ED 442141)

Hennings, D. G. (2002). *Communication in action: Teaching literature-based language arts.* Boston: Houghton Mifflin.

Herrmann, B. A. (1988). Two approaches for helping poor readers become more strategic. *The Reading Teacher, 41,* 24–28.

Hoffman, J. V. (1998). When bad things happen to good ideas in literacy education: Professional dilemmas, personal decisions, and political traps. *The Reading Teacher, 52,* 102–112.

Honig, B., Diamond, L., Gutlohn, L., & Mahler, J. (2000). *Teaching reading: Sourcebook for kindergarten through eighth grade.* Novato, CA: Arena Press.

Hurford, D. P., & Sanders, R. E. (1990). Assessment and remediation of a phonemic discrimination deficit in reading disabled second and fourth graders. *Journal of Experimental Child Psychology, 50,* 396–415.

ICTS. (1996). *Study Guide: Language Arts.* Illinois State Board of Education and National Evaluation Systems, Inc.

Invernizzi, M. A., Abouzeid, M. P., & Bloodgood, J. W. (1997). Integrated word study: Spelling, grammar, and meaning in the language arts classroom. *Language Arts, 74,* 185–192.

Irwin, J. (1991). *Teaching reading comprehension processes,* 2nd ed. Boston: Allyn & Bacon.

Jackson, C. W., & Larkin, M. J. (2002). Rubric: Teaching students to use grading rubrics. *Teaching Exceptional Children, 35,* 40–47.

Johnson, D. W., & Johnson, R. T. (1984). *Circles of learning: Cooperation in the classroom.* Alexandria, VA: Association for Supervision and Curriculum Development.

Johnson, D. W., & Johnson, R. T. (1989/1990). Social skills for successful work groups. *Educational Leadership, 29–33.*

Johnson, K. (1979). Communicative approaches and communicative processes. In C. J. Brumfit & J. Johnson (Eds.), *The communicative approach to language teaching.* Oxford, England: Oxford University Press.

Joseph, L. M. (1998/1999). Word boxes help children with learning disabilities identify and spell words. *The Reading Teacher, 52,* 348–356.

Joseph, L. M., (2000a). Using word boxes as a large group phonics approach in a first grade classroom. *Reading Horizons, 41,* 117–127.

Joseph, L. M. (2000b). Developing first graders' phonemic awareness, word identification, and spelling: A comparison of two contemporary phonic instructional approaches. *Reading Research and Instruction, 39,* 160–169.

Kagan, S. (1986). *Cooperative learning: Resources for teachers.* San Juan Capistrano, CA: Resources for Teachers.

Kibby, M. W. (1989). Teaching sight vocabulary with and without context before silent reading: A field test of the "focus of attention" hypothesis. *Journal of Reading Behavior, 21,* 261–277.

Kinnucan-Welch, K. K., Magill, D., & Dean, M. (1999). Strategic teaching and strategic learning in first-grade classrooms. *Reading Horizons, 40,* 2–21.

Klinger, J. K, & Vaughn, S. (1999). Promoting reading comprehension, content learning, and English acquisition through collaborative strategic reading (CSR). *The Reading Teacher, 52,* 738–747.

Krashen, S. (1982). *Principles and practice in second language acquisition.* Oxford, England: Pergamon Press.

Krashen, S. (1993). *The power of reading.* Englewood, NJ: Libraries United.

Krashen, S. & Terrell, T. (1983). *The natural approach: Language acquisition in the classroom.* Oxford, England: Pergamon Press.

Kucan, L., & Beck, I. L. (1997). Thinking aloud and reading comprehension research: Inquiry, instruction, and social interaction. *Review of Educational Research, 67,* 271–299.

Laing, S. P., & Kamki, A. G. (2002). The use of think-aloud protocols to compare inferencing abilities in average and below average readers. *Journal of Learning Disabilities, 35,* 436–447.

Langer, J. A. (1981). From theory to practice: A prereading plan. *Journal of Reading, 24,* 152–156.

Larsen-Freeman, D., & Long, M. H. (1991). *An introduction to second language acquisition research.* New York: Longman.

Lee, D. M., & Allen, R. V. (1963). *Learning to read through experience,* 2nd ed. New York: Meredith.

Leseman, P. P., & de Jong, P. F. (1998). Home literacy: Opportunity, instruction, cooperation, and social-emotional quality predicting early reading development. *Reading Research Quarterly, 33,* 294–318.

Lessow-Hurley, J. (1990). *The foundations of dual language instruction.* White Plains, NJ: Longman.

Lewis, M., Wray, D., & Rospigliosi, P. (1994). ...And I want it in your own words. *The Reading Teacher, 47,* 528–536.

Lloyd, C. V. (1998). Engaging students at the top (without leaving the rest behind). *Journal of Adolescent & Adult Literacy, 42,* 184–191.

Manzo, A. V. (1975). Guided reading procedure. *Journal of Reading, 19,* 287–291.

Maria, K. (1990). *Reading comprehension instruction: Issues and strategies.* Timonium, NY: New York Press.

Mastropieri, M. A., & Scruggs, T. E. (1997). Best practices in promoting reading comprehension in students with learning disabilities. *Remedial and Special Education, 18,* 197–213.

McCauley, J. K., & McCauley, D. S. (1992). Using choral reading to promote language learning for ESL students. *The Reading Teacher, 45,* 526–534.

McIntosh, M. E., & Draper, R. J. (1995). Applying the question-answer relationship strategy in mathematics. *Journal of Adolescent & Adult Literacy, 39,* 120–131.

McKenzie, G. R. (1979). Data charts: A crutch for helping pupils organize reports. *Language Arts, 56,* 784–788.

McNinch, G. H. (1981). A method for teaching sight words to disabled readers. *The Reading Teacher, 34,* 269–272.

Merkley, D. M., & Jefferies, D. (2000/2001). Guidelines for implementing a graphic organizer. *The Reading Teacher, 54,* 350–357.

Mesmer, H. A. (2001). Decodable text: A review of what we know. *Reading Research and Instruction, 40,* 121–142.

Mesmer, H. A., & Hutchins, E. J. (2002). Using QARs with charts and graphs. *The Reading Teacher, 56,* 20–29.

Meyers, M. (1993). *Teaching to diversity: Teaching and learning in the multi-ethnic classroom.* Toronto: Irwin Publishing.

Miller, T. (1998). The place of picture books in middle-level classroom. *Journal of Adolescent & Adult Literacy, 41,* 376–381.

Mitchell, J. P., Abernathy, T. V., & Gowans, L. P. (1998). Making sense of literacy portfolios: A four step plan. *Journal of Adolescent & Adult Literacy, 41,* 384–389.

Morris, D. (1982). "Word sort": A categorization strategy for improving word recognition ability. *Reading Psychology: An International Quarterly, 3,* 247–259.

Master Reading Teacher Preparation Manual. (2002–2003). Retrieved May 21, 2003 from http://www.texmat.nesinc.com/PDFs/MRTPrepManual.pdf

MTEL. (2002–2003). *2002–2003 Registration Bulletin.* Massachusetts Department of Education and National Evaluation Systems, Inc.

MTTC. (2001). *Study Guide,* Vol. 2. Michigan State Board of Education and National Evaluation Systems, Inc.

Nagy, W. E. (1998). *Teaching vocabulary to improve reading comprehension.* Urbana, IL: National Council of Teachers.

Nation, K., & Hulme, C. (1997). Phonemic segmentation, not onset-rime segmentation, predicts early reading and spelling skills. *Reading Research Quarterly, 32,* 154–167.

NESINC. (2001). *MTTC study guide,* Vol. 2—language arts. NESINC.

Newell, J. (1984). Advance Organizers: Their construction and use in instructional development. ERIC Document ED 298908.

NYSTCE. (2000). *Assessment of Teaching Skills—Written Preparation Guide.* The University of the State of New York/New York State Department of Education/ National Evaluation Systems, Inc.

Ogle, D. M. (1986). K-W-L: A teaching model that develops active reading of expository text. *The Reading Teacher, 39,* 564–571.

O'Grady, W., Dobrovolsky, M., & Arnoff, M. (1993). *Contemporary linguistics: An introduction,* 2nd ed. New York: St. Martin's Press.

Olsen, A., & Ames, W. (1972). *Teaching reading skills in secondary schools.* Scranton, PA: Intext Educational Publishers, *as quoted in* R. T. Vacca & J. Vacca. (1989). *Content area reading.* Glenview, IL: Scott, Foresman.

O'Mally, E. (Ed.). (1998). *Reading/Language Arts Framework for California Public Schools, Kindergarten Through Grade Twelve.* Sacramento: California Department of Education.

OSAT. (2001). *Study Guide,* Vol. 1. Oklahoma Commission for Teacher Preparation and National Evaluation Systems, Inc.

Osgood, J., & Colon, R. J. (1998). Legal responsibilities toward students with disabilities: What every administrator should know. *Bulletin: Special Education,* 40–54.

Palincsar, A. S., & Brown, A. L. (1986). Interactive teaching to promote independent learning from text. *The Reading Teacher, 39,* 771–777.

Park, B. (1982). The big book trend—A discussion with Don Holdaway. *Language Arts, 59,* 814–821.

Pearson, P. D., & Dole, J. A. (1987). Explicit comprehension instruction: A review of research and a new conceptualization of instruction. *Elementary School Journal, 88,* 151–165.

Penny, L. G. (2002). Teaching decoding skills to poor readers in high school. *Journal of Literacy Research, 34,* 99–118.

Peregoy, S., & Boyle, O. (1993). *Reading, writing, and learning in ESL: A resource book for K-8 teachers.* White Plains, NY: Longman.

Perez, S. A. (2000). Teaching second language learners in the regular classroom. *Reading Improvement, 37,* 45–48.

PLACE Study Guide, Vol. 2. (2001). Colorado Department of Education and National Evaluation Systems, Inc.

Pressley, M., Brown, R., Beard El-Dinary, P., & Afflerbach, P. (1995). The comprehension instruction that students need: Instruction fostering constructively responsive reading. *Learning Disabilities Research, 10,* 215–224.

Rakes, G. C., Rakes, T. A., & Smith, L. J. (1995). Using visuals to enhance secondary students' reading comprehension of expository text. *Journal of Adolescent & Adult Literacy, 39,* 46–54.

Raphael, T. E. (1982). Question-answering strategies for children. *The Reading Teacher, 35,* 186–191.

Rasinski, T. V. (2000). Speed does matter in reading. *The Reading Teacher, 54,* 146–151.

Rhodes, L., & Nathenson-Mejia, S. (1993). Anecdotal records: A powerful tool for ongoing literacy assessment. *The Reading Teacher, 46,* 503–509.

RICA. (2002–2003). RICA *Registration Bulletin 2002–2003.* California Commission on Teacher Credentialing and National Evaluation Systems, Inc.

Rogers, D. B. (1984). Assessing study skills. *Journal of Reading, 28,* 346–354.

Rosenshine, B., & Meister, C. (1994). Reciprocal teaching: A review of the research. *Review of Educational Research, 64,* 479–530.

Rosner, N. L., Hoffman, J. V., & Farest, C. (1990). Language, literature, and at-risk children. *The Reading Teacher, 43,* 554–559.

Rupley, W. H., Logan, J. W., & Nichols, W. D. (1998/1999). Vocabulary instruction in a balanced reading program. *The Reading Teacher, 52,* 336–346.

Samuels, S. J. (1967). Attention processing in reading: The effect of pictures in the acquisition of reading responses. *Journal of Educational Psychology, 58,* 337–342.

Samuels, S. J. (1997). The method of repeated readings. *The Reading Teacher, 50,* 376–381.

Sanders, N. M. (1966). *Classroom questions: What kinds?* New York: Harper & Row.

Schatz, E. K. (1986). Context clues are unreliable predictors of word meanings. *Reading Research Quarterly, 21,* 438–453.

Schefelbine, J. L. (1990). Student factors related to variability in learning word meanings from context. *Journal of Reading Behavior, 22,* 71–97.

Schlagal, R. C., & Schlagal, J. H. (1992). The integral character of spelling: Teaching strategies for multiple purposes. *Language Arts, 69,* 418–423.

Schwantes, F. M. (1991). Children's use of semantic and syntactic information for word recognition and determination of sentence meaningfulness. *Journal of Reading Behavior, 23,* 335–350.

Serafini, F. (2000/2001). Three paradigms of assessment: Measurement, procedure, and inquiry. *The Reading Teacher, 54,* 384–393.

Shanahan, T. (1997). Reading-writing relationship, thematic units, inquiry learning…in pursuit of effective integrated literacy instruction. *The Reading Teaching, 51,* 12–19.

Shanahan, T. (1988). The reading-writing relationship: Seven instructional principles. *The Reading Teacher, 41,* 636–647.

Shanahan, T., & Shanahan, S. (1997). Character perspective charting: Helping children develop a more complete conception of story. *The Reading Teacher, 50,* 668–677.

Simpson, M. L., Hayes, C. G., Stahl, N., Connor, R. I., & Weaver, D. (1988). An initial validation of a study strategy system. *Journal of Reading Behavior, 20,* 149–180.

Stahl, S. A. (1985). To teach a word well: A framework for vocabulary instruction. *Reading World, 24,* 16–22.

Stahl, S. A. (1992). Saying the "p" word: Nine guidelines for exemplary phonics instruction. *The Reading Teacher, 45,* 618–625.

Stahl, S. A., Duffy-Hester, A. M., & Dougherty-Stahl, K. A. (1998). Everything you wanted to know about phonics (but were afraid to ask). *Reading Research Quarterly, 33,* 338–355.

Stahl, S. A., & Kuhn, M. R. (2002). Making it sound like language: Developing fluency. *The Reading Teacher, 55,* 582–584.

Stahl, S. A., & Shiel, T. G. (1992). Teaching meaning vocabulary: Productive approaches for poor readers. *Reading and Writing Quarterly: Overcoming Learning Difficulties, 8,* 223–241.

Stieglitz, E. L., & Stieglitz, V. S. (1981). SAVOR the word to reinforce vocabulary in the content areas. *Journal of Reading, 25,* 46–51.

Sutton, C. (1989). Helping the nonnative English speaker with reading. *The Reading Teacher, 42,* 684–688.

Swanborn, M. S. L., & de Glopper, K. (1999). Incidental word learning while reading: A meta-analysis. *Review of Educational Research, 69,* 261–285.

Tadlock, D. F. (1978). SQ3R—Why it works, based on an information processing theory of learning. *Journal of Reading, 22,* 110–113.

Taylor, M. (1992). The language experience approach and adult learners. National Centers for ESL Instruction (ERIC Document Reproduction Service EDO-LE-92-01). http://www.cal.org/ncle/digest/lang_exper. html (May 21, 2003).

TExES/ExCET Registration Bulletin (2002–2003). Retrieved May 21, 2003 from http://www.excet.nesinc. com/TE_20022003RegBulletin.pdf

Tompkins, G. (2003). *Literacy for the 21st century,* 3rd ed. Englewood Cliffs, NJ: Prentice Hall.

Townsend, M. A. R., & Clarihew, A. (1989). Facilitating children's comprehension through the use of advanced organizers. *Journal of Reading Behavior, 21,* 15–36.

Trelease, J. (1995). Sustained silent reading. *California English, 1,* 8–9.

Tunmer, W. E., & Nesdale, A. R. (1988). Phoneme segmentation skills and learning to read. *Journal of Educational Psychology, 77,* 417–427.

Vacca, R. T., & Vacca, J. L., (1989). *Content area reading,* 3rd ed. Glenview, IL: Scott, Foresman.

Vacca, R. T., Vacca, J. L., Grove, M. K., Burkey, L., Lenhart, L. A., & McKeon, C. (2003). *Reading and Learning to Read,* 5th ed. Boston: Allyn & Bacon.

Vickery, K. S., Reynolds, V. A., & Cochran, S. W. (1987). Multisensory training approach for reading, spelling, and handwriting: Orton-Gillingham based curriculum in a public school setting. *Annals of Dyslexia, 37,* 189–200.

Wagstaff, J. M. (1997/1998). Building practical knowledge of letter-sound correspondences: A beginner's word wall and beyond. *The Reading Teacher, 51,* 298–304.

Whaley, J. F. (1981). Story grammars and reading instruction. *The Reading Teacher, 34,* 762–771.

White, T. G., Power, M. A., & White, S. (1989). Morphological analysis: Implications for teaching and understanding vocabulary growth. *Reading Research Quarterly, 24,* 283–304.

White, T. G., & Yanagihara, A. (1989). Teaching elementary students to use word-part clues. *The Reading Teacher, 42,* 302–308.

Williams, J. P. (1980). Teaching decoding with an emphasis on phoneme analysis and phoneme blending. *Journal of Educational Psychology, 72,* 1–15.

Woden, P. E., & Boettcher, W. (1990). Young children's acquisition of alphabet knowledge. *Journal of Reading Behavior, 22,* 277–295.

Wysocki, K., & Jenkins, J. R. (1987). Deriving word meanings through morphological generalization. *Reading Research Quarterly, 22,* 66–81.

Yanok, J. (1988). Individualized instruction: A good approach. *Academic Therapy, 24,* 162–167.

Yokota, J. (1993). Issues in selecting multicultural children's literature. *Language Arts, 70,* 156–166.

Yokota, J., & Yopp, R. H. (2000). Supporting phonemic awareness development in the classroom. *The Reading Teacher, 54,* 130–143.

Yopp, H. K. (1992). Developing phonemic awareness in young children. *The Reading Teacher, 45,* 696–703.

Zutell, J. (1998). Word sorting: A developmental spelling approach to word study for delayed readers. *Reading & Writing Quarterly: Overcoming Learning Difficulties, 14,* 219–238.